ALLEGIANCE

TO

GOD AND CORPS

ALLEGIANCE TO GOD AND CORPS

The Life Experiences of a Military Muslim

HAFIZ NAIM ALI CAMP

Trafford Publishing
Bloomington, IN

Order this book online at www.trafford.com
or email orders@trafford.com

Most Trafford titles are also available at major online book retailers.

Printed in the United States of America.

ISBN: 978-1-4269-5822-9 (sc)
ISBN: 978-1-4269-5823-6 (hc)
ISBN: 978-1-4269-5824-3 (e)

Library of Congress Control Number: 2011902488

Trafford rev. 02/24/2011

www.trafford.com

North America & international
toll-free: 1 888 232 4444 (USA & Canada)
phone: 250 383 6864 • fax: 812 355 4082

A RESPECTFUL DEDICATION:

This book is dedicated to my Father, the late **Retired Master Sergeant Rudolph Edwin Camp**, who also served this country with 30 years of faithful service in the U. S. Army. Through his attributes, he was able to affect the lives of many people. His humble and caring demeanor was infectious for those he interacted with. From my knowledge and those who surrounded him, he was always a man of heart, compassion, and good character.

PREFACE

This memoir explores the life experiences of a United States Marine who reverted to Islam when he was a Staff Sergeant (SSgt) in 1994. He shares 16 years of experiences-positive and negative-and his devotion to God, as he dedicated 30 years of faithful service to the Corps.

During those 16 years, he took advantage of the opportunity to meet diverse groups of people, Muslim and non-Muslim, from all over the world and to share stories about their families and cultures. Two countries that had the largest impact on his writing were Palestine and Bosnia because of the atrocities their people have withstood under the ruling forces that governed that territory. He recalls first-hand stories from two Bosnian brothers who are now Marines, who fought in the Bosnian War as teenagers. He also has a close family relationship with a Palestinian family whose three sons have served in the Corps.

The writer also talks about his relationships and experiences with six military Muslim Chaplains, from the Navy, Air Force, and Army, all of which can give you a vivid picture of what it's like being a Muslim in the military and the challenges they faced during the course of their duties.

Lastly, he writes about the tragic 9/11, Ft Hood, and controversial Ground Zero Masjid incidents that have had a devastating impact on Muslim communities world-wide and the efforts that many Muslims exhausted to show the world that it was not the religion that committed those acts, but merely individuals trying to use the religion to justify their agendas.

ACKNOWLEDGMENTS

Although the names are not mentioned in this memoir, I would like to acknowledge those who shared these experiences with me. The names of those who captured my memory while constructing this memoir will be forever embedded in my mind and in my heart. I intentionally withheld all names from this work except for my father's the late **Rudolph Edwin Camp,** my son's, **Michel Andre' Camp**, and my grandson's, **Idris Naim Siddiq Camp.** A special acknowledgement goes out to my wife and daughters who encouraged and inspired me to put these special moments of my life in writing. They were my best critics during the year it took me to write it.

MY ALLEGIANCE

My foremost Allegiance is to God, Creator and Sustainer of the universe. I worship Him and I worship Him alone without partners of any sort. I submit to do His will and to be an example for believers and non-believers to remind them of the Day of Judgment. My duties and responsibilities to the Creator are to worship Him alone, to follow the five pillars of Islam, adhere to the seven principles of Islam and to exemplify the character of His Messenger, the Prophet Muhammad (Pbuh), through his Sunnah, or way of life.

I also have an Allegiance to the United States Marine Corps and to the men and women I have served with, along with those that served before me and those that will serve after me. The Corps was the vehicle through which I served my country, defending it against all enemies, both foreign and domestic. The Corps has provided for my family for the past 30 years, and has given us the opportunity to travel and see the world. It has enabled us to meet many wonderful people, to share their cultures, and has taught us to appreciate the freedom we have as Americans.

CONTENTS

Chapter One

THE FEW, THE PROUD, THE MARINES

While attending Virginia State College (VSC)-now Virginia State University of Petersburg, Virginia-I made a critical decision that changed the course of my life. High above the banks of the Appomattox River, I was about to embark on a lifetime journey that most could only imagine.

A year after graduating from high school in 1977, I was accepted to Virginia State College. At this point, I was faced with the option to attend Virginia State or stay close to home with a dead end job. After reviewing all of my options, I quickly made the decision to make VSC the institution that would prepare me for my future. What swayed my decision were the facts that I had many friends who were already enrolled there, it was a Historically Black College/University (HBCU), and that it was only an hour and a half away from home. This way, if I were to get homesick it wouldn't take long for me to get back to the comforts of where I was raised. Unable to afford a car, I would have to rely on friends to make that quick trip down the back roads of Williamsburg, Virginia to see my loved ones. My first month of school, I went home every weekend. My neighborhood friend that I rode with had been doing it for two years so I didn't feel bad. Although I enjoyed going home, I had to slowly wean myself from making the trip so frequently.

It was at VSC where I experienced my first time being away from home, out on my own, making my own decisions. Although frightening at first, I adapted well and made the best of my experience. While there for orientation a month earlier, the orientation staff related about many who were unable to cope with being away from home in a college environment. I definitely did not want to fall in this category because I had the obligation and opportunity to be the first in my family to graduate from college.

My father, **Rudolph Edwin Camp**, enlisted in the U. S. Army directly after high school. He had a wonderful career of 30 years, with tours in Korea and Vietnam. He was proud to serve in the military that provided his family with a suitable lifestyle. It also provided our family the opportunity to experience France, Germany, and a few different states. After retiring from the Army, he worked as a security guard at Ft. Eustis, a nearby Army Base located in Newport News, Virginia. Although very intelligent, Dad never went to college and I never heard him talk about it either. He spent most of his youthful days in a small country county called Amelia located about an hour from Richmond, Virginia. I recall telling him that I wanted to go to college and he confidently told me that he would make financial arrangements so that I would be able to go. Quiet most of the time and always reading fictional books, he didn't ask what I would major in and he didn't know if I had researched the school or not.

My mother, the oldest of thirteen children was forced to drop out of high school after the eleventh grade. Marriage and the birth of my oldest brother ended her high school career. I can recall the earlier days while my dad was overseas how she would take us to our grandmother's before she headed off to work. We spent many days at our grandmother's place and most of those days turned into nights. We loved going there because it gave us a lot more to do than staying at our home. Grandma, as we called her, would have us chop wood for the stove, feed the hunting dogs or run errands back and forth to the store. She kept a house full of children, most of them being grand and great grandchildren. It seemed like she could never turn us away regardless of how tired she was. She often fell asleep with a grandchild in her arms. My mother's brothers and sisters had the same idea because in most cases their children would end up there also. We all blended in with my cousins who were always there. Time spent at my grandmother's allowed us all to bond. With a long line of aunts and uncles in that family, I have two aunts and one uncle who are younger than I am.

I guess that working nights and raising four children never gave mom the opportunity to further her education. Even after my father returned from overseas, she worked and focused on her primary role of making sure that us children had what we needed. Mom retired after twenty years of service at the Ft. Eustis Exchange. Between my three siblings and I-me being the second oldest-my older brother opted not to go to college because he was not offered a scholarship after four years of football at Denbigh High School in Newport News, Virginia. A year after graduation, he traveled to Washington, D.C. to try out for the Washington Redskins. He was not successful in that endeavor and later joined the U. S. Army in search of a stable career.

It was at VSC where I was exposed to many people from so many cities and states. The majority of the enrollment at VSC came from the east coast, although there were a few students that came from as far away as California, and one young lady was from Bermuda. It was really strange to me to see how so many of the students gravitated toward the students from New York City and Washington, D.C. The students from these two cities were apparently the trend setters and everyone wanted to emulate them. They were up on all the new fashions and they knew the hip lingo.

It was so interesting for me to talk with students from different states and countries because it gave me a perspective on how it was growing up in their environments. Many of the conversations I couldn't relate to because I had never been exposed to some of the things mentioned in their stories. I heard stories about catching the train over to Madison Square Garden to see the New York Knicks play, or about attending cultural events. I heard stories about shopping in the fashion districts and shopping in stores like Macy's and Saks Fifth Avenue. I often heard stories of trying foods from Russia, Greece, and the Middle East, and seeing stars and famous personalities right out on city streets. Unfortunately, my upbringing in Newport News, Virginia sheltered me from those types of cultural experiences. I could only offer stories of swimming, roller skating, and watching movies at Ft. Eustis. Although we had a blast growing up, these were the highlights of my neighborhood.

I was able to turn a few heads when I mentioned that I had lived in France and Germany for a few years. My father was stationed in Verdun, France where my younger brother and I were born. My birth certificate is written entirely in French and no, I wasn't given dual French and American citizenship. I have no memory of anything we did there because we left France when I was three years old. My father took us back to Verdun while we were stationed at Ramstein Air Force Base, Germany in 1968, to show us where we lived. France and Germany became my topics of discussion because that was the only way that I could conger up any interest whenever we sat down to socialize. Newport News, Virginia could not provide me enough material to compete with the stories told by the other students from the larger and more popular cities.

It was at VSC where I was exposed to social organizations, fraternities, and sororities. While in high school, I heard stories from some of those who pledged these organizations, some of them at VSC. At that time, it seemed like the male college students from my neighborhood were pledging either Groove Phi Groove Social Fellowship Incorporated or the Men of Crimson and Cream, which I'll use instead of the fraternity's name for legality reasons. Some of my high school friends and I were so enthused about pledging, we would attend house parties shouting the names of the organizations we were interested in. I figured that I would get to campus and research both organizations to see which one I would be compatible with and which was doing the most for the communities. I also wanted to pledge hard because I had heard that the harder you pledge, the more you'll love the organization. Pledging hard means to endure the hardest mental and physical treatment you can tolerate from those who are pledging you.

When I arrived on campus for orientation, I made it one of my priorities to talk to members of both organizations to get a feel of who I would be dealing with when I decided to pledge. The brothers of Groove Phi Groove Social Fellowship Incorporated appeared to be the gangsters of the campus. There was something about them that attracted a lot of interest but with that interest came the fear of how much of a physical and mental challenge I would have to endure to become a member. With nicknames like Rock Monster, Jesse James and Mandingo, it was very intimidating just thinking about pledging that organization, however, I was already leaning toward that group due to influence from my high school basketball coach's son, who had pledged Groove Phi Groove, SFI at Virginia Tech. He used to come to our weekend practices during holidays. Although I never talked with him about it, I watched how he carried himself and I particularly noted the respect he showed to his father, the assistant coaches, and staff.

In 1978, I had the opportunity to watch my first Trojan Chapter line of Groove Phi Groove pledge. Through our National Headquarters in Silver Spring, Maryland, Virginia State was recognized as the Trojan Chapter, coming from the mascot of the school. Each chapter of Groove Phi Groove was named in the same manner. I often saw the three pledges, called Swanxmen, running across campus in line with white t-shirts, blue jeans, combat boots and green Army field jackets. I watched them when they came to the cafeteria for dinner. The "Caf" was where students congregated in the evenings after class. It was the hub of the campus located in the center of the male and female dormitories. Although the food was not too good, it stayed filled to capacity until it closed. I would watch the Swanxmen as the big brothers sent them on errand after errand, carrying books and trays, getting phone numbers, and passing out chewing gum to whomever they were told. It seemed like they didn't get an opportunity to eat most of the time. They always appeared tired, they never smiled and they responded very quickly to everything the brothers uttered. It was so intriguing how the pledges would get so embarrassed and humiliated and they still did all they could to please the brothers.

In fall of 1978, I joined the "MIGs," (Men Interested in Groove) and we began raising money and preparing to go through the pledging process. Two or three times a week we walked through the dorms selling hot dogs and candy to offset the cost of material we needed for the pledging process or "going on line." We concentrated on the late hours knowing that everyone would then be hungry after the cafeteria food wore off. We had about 15 MIGs and the majority of them were from the Northeast. The organization had a Rush at the Student Union Building to see how much interest they had for joining the fellowship. A Rush is a semi-formal gathering by fraternities and social organizations to see how many students are interested in pledging. They explain the history of the organization and they display academic and community awareness. All of this was basically a report card on how and what the organization was doing. They also answered questions for those who were curious. They were overwhelmed with the number of students interested. My next priority was to make sure that I had the grade point average of at least a 2.0 to qualify for initiation. At that time I had a 3.2 GPA.

I chose not to pledge the Men of Crimson and Cream mainly because they thought that they were the pretty boys of the campus. That definitely was not my image. They had many brothers on campus and were known for having many students pledge at one time. I could see their caliber of brothers though. One student from my neighborhood pledged that organization. We used to take his lunch money from him in high school, and watched him do nothing as we walked away. They were more concerned about the quantity of pledges and not the quality of pledges that they were bringing into the organization.

In January of 1979, I decided to take my chance at initiation. I submitted my letter to the President of the organization explaining why I wanted to pledge and what I had to offer the fellowship. They were very pleased with my letter. I made it known to the organization that I wanted to pledge and they informed me that they would let me know if I was accepted. One week later I was told to put on a suit and meet at one of the brother's apartments off campus for the induction into the pledge process. There were eight of us that showed up for the induction. The other seven didn't have the grade point average or they backed down at the last minute because of fear or they just weren't ready to make the sacrifice. We were warned that pledging Groove Phi Groove was no joke. The brothers wouldn't give us first-hand stories, fearing that we would change our minds but a few of my neighborhood Grooves gave me a first-hand description of what to expect. One of them had pledged at VSC three years prior.

All eight of us were blind-folded and led one by one into a dark room for the induction ceremony. From that night on, we were officially called "Swanxmen," pledges for Groove Phi Groove Social Fellowship Incorporated. For the next eight weeks we would be subjected to physical and mental torment, humiliation, and sleep deprivation. We lost four Swanxmen the first week and one in the second. They couldn't tolerate the mental and physical requirements. With three of us left, the next six weeks would prove to be a test by all means. We did everything imaginable during this pledging process from passing raw eggs from mouth to mouth, and eating raw onions like apples, to running around campus with paper bags over our head calling ourselves space invaders.

Due to the lack of focus and sleep deprivation, my grades started to suffer. Although we were required to attend the library every night to study, I found myself sleeping at the library and neglecting my studies. Some of the brothers came through the library to check on us. I remember falling asleep in trigonometry class and getting hit in the back of my head by erasers from one of the brothers in my class. He strategically sat behind me because he knew that I would have problems staying awake. At week six I decided to drop line in an effort to salvage my grades and I vowed to return the next semester to pledge again. The brothers were disappointed that I dropped the initiation. I guess I had shown them that I had potential and that I would've been an asset to the organization.

I felt bad for the one Swanxman that I had left on line. The last two weeks he had to fend for himself, vulnerable to a group of brothers who were very energetic and imaginative. I had to do it, though, because my grades were the priority and I was in school to get my education and not to pledge. I would rebound the next semester. A few of my friends mentioned that if I pledged via a graduate chapter, the pledging process would be a lot easier. Those that were scared to pledge undergrad pledged the graduate route. The graduate brothers have jobs and families and they really don't have the time to put into pledging. Basically, you pay your pledging and annual dues, learn the history of the organization, do a few community projects, and you're in. The twist of pledging the graduate route is that many undergraduate brothers don't respect the brothers that pledge the graduate route because they feel that they entered the organization too easily. There is no way that I would've taken that route. I wanted the real challenge of undergraduate pledging.

When I returned to State in the fall of 1979, the organization didn't have an initiation period or line, but in the spring of 1980 they did. This was my opportunity to redeem myself. I basically went through the same procedure as the previous year. The only thing different was that this time I knew what to expect. I was asked by a few of the brothers if I was going to drop this time around and I told them that if they didn't plan on killing me then I would make it. The "Sole Survivor" of the last line told me that he was going to make it extremely hard for me because I left him hanging the first time. This was the name that the brothers gave him because he was the only Swanxman to cross the burning sands into the organization out of the eight of us. I was totally prepared to go the distance, regardless of what I had to endure. I had to go through an entire last summer explaining to inquirers why I didn't make it the first time. I found it very uncomfortable explaining why I had dropped to visiting brothers who had traveled from other schools to see me while I was on line the first time. To them I was an "Eternal Swanxman," and I would remain one until I pledged again and made it. I was pledged this time by two brothers that went to high school with me. One pledged there at VSC and the other at Hampton Institute, now Hampton University.

Pledging was even harder the second time around and if it wasn't for the help of our line sweethearts, or "Precious Gems," it would've been a lot worse. The Precious Gems were a female auxiliary group to the organization that helped to make the pledging process easier.

They purchased food for us, helped us with our assignments, raised money for us, and scolded the brothers when they felt that they were too hard on us. The Precious Gems also planned our going over party and helped us celebrate. A going over party is a party to help celebrate the completion of the pledge period. We also received help from some of the sisters of our sister organization, Swing Phi Swing Social Fellowship Incorporated. We had one sister that worked at the store at the bottom of the hill on the front campus, and she gave us incredible discounts. At times she wouldn't charge us at all.

On March 28th, 1980, I crossed the burning sands and was inducted into the organization. I got "Gs" branded on both arms the next day. Most black social organizations and fraternities brand their arms and legs with their organizational symbols to show they've made the sacrifice of pledging. Most brothers were drunk before getting branded. I didn't drink so I had to take mine without the aid of any type of pain reducer. I don't think that there were any brothers without a "G" branded or tattooed on their arms or legs. Some have multiple Gs. A week later I went home for the weekend. My mother saw the brands on my arms and asked if I was crazy. She had no idea of what I went through to earn those Gs. Groove Phi until the day I die!

Virginia State College was also where I met the woman that would later become my wife. I met her in the cafeteria while she and a couple of friends came in to eat dinner. From time to time I would find her staring at me and smiling, often telling her friends to look at me. I immediately made it known that I was interested in her and it was then when our relationship started. I soon began walking her to class and spending time with her every opportunity I could. She had a wonderful personality, a very good upbringing, and she had no strings attached to any male friends. She was from Suffolk, Virginia, a small city in southern Virginia located about ten miles from the North Carolina border. Growing up I heard about the

Suffolk Raceway that was one of the attractions of the city. Suffolk was also known for its Planters Peanut and Lipton Tea factories that employed a large number of its residents. I considered her a country girl but she wasn't exactly from the country.

Life at VSC exposed me to a young lady from New Jersey that really seemed different from the others there. This young lady played on the VSC women's basketball team and, unlike the others, she wore long pants on the court and she always covered her hair. I would watch them practice in the heat of the summer and her attire never changed. She was the first Muslim that I had come in contact with. I, like everyone else wondered why she wore the long pants and scarf all the time. Her teammates told us that she was Muslim and that Muslim women had to dress modestly to guard their body parts against roaming eyes with bad intentions. College was one place where it's about letting it all hang out when it comes to the opposite sex. Promiscuity ran rampant on college campuses, and neither my friends nor I could understand why this young Muslim woman would dare to be different from everyone else on the campus. My freshmen crew and I, along with most upperclassmen, would pick out the most popular routes on campus and would sit and watch the half dressed women walk back and forth across the campus giggling when they saw us watching. During the winter months we were deprived of the treat but in the summer and fall we made up for it. During my freshman year, hot pants and halter tops were still popular and that was perfectly alright with the male population on campus. Little did I know that seventeen years later, I would learn to appreciate the modesty displayed by this young Muslim woman.

During my junior year, I began to lose interest in school. I used the fellowship, and social life to deter me from attending class, which resulted in academic probation. My grades had suffered again from pledging and now I had to pay the consequences. I never told my parents that I was on academic probation and I stayed at school although I was not enrolled in school the upcoming semester. While not enrolled in school, I spent most of my days on campus at the Student Union Building playing table tennis and socializing. After a month or so it got old. I felt that I was wasting my life away while everyone else was preparing theirs for the future. I needed an outlet.

While walking to campus from downtown one morning, I discovered a U. S. Marine Corps brochure with a Marine in Dress Blues on the cover. Dress Blues are the Marine's formal uniform worn only on formal occasions. Regardless of what it had to say on the inside, I was focused on that uniform. I thought about how I would look in it. Being affiliated with the military all of my life, I never saw a uniform that impressive. The black coat and the high rise collar with the metallic gold eagle, globe and anchors were appealing. The red blood stripe that's worn down the trouser seam complimented the uniform well and the white cover and gloves really set if off. I kept the brochure and pulled it out of my back pocket every now and then to take another look at that uniform. When I returned to the apartment that night, I actually read the inside of the brochure to see what the Marine Corps had to offer. From what I read on the inside, they offered the opportunity to travel, to learn a technical skill and obtain money for college. This didn't seem too bad, especially the part about money for college. Although my parents never mentioned it, my tuition put them in financial burden. I recall calling home about a month prior to ask mom to send me money. She replied that she had to cash in a few of her savings bonds and then she would send the cash. I was devastated after I heard this and I immediately began looking for sources to obtain money for school. All efforts were to no avail.

I already owed on one student loan and there was no way that I was going to apply for another. I began to contemplate going in to talk to the recruiter. While on campus the next day, I showed the brochure to my fellow students for some feedback. The uniform caught the eyes of everyone, but one of my brothers in particular. He also read the paragraph that mentioned the Marines having a reserve program where you only had to participate one weekend a month and two weeks in the summer. The following day we went to talk with the recruiter.

As we walked into the recruiting station, we saw Marine Corps paraphernalia everywhere. Posters and stickers covered the walls and the sound of drill cadence echoed throughout the station. They were listening to tapes of Marine Corps drill instructors as they marched their platoons on the parade deck. We watched the videos of the recruits engaging the obstacle course and qualifying with their rifles on the rifle range. It was so motivating to watch these videos and I could see myself accepting the challenge to be one of the Few, the Proud, the Marines. It was an easy decision for me because I wasn't enrolled in school at that time and I was wasting my life away. There I was after two and a half years of Army R.O.T.C. ready to enlist into the Marine Corps. I was passing up my opportunity to become an Army Officer and enlisting in the Marine Corps. Some of my classmates from the R.O.T.C. cadets thought that I would regret the decision.

We sat down with the recruiter and asked what type of jobs the Corps had to offer. He said that we would have to take the ASVAB (Armed Services Vocational Aptitude Battery) test and whatever area we scored the highest in would be the area where we probably would excel. We offered to go to the testing center in Richmond to take the test. About a week later we were called back by the recruiter and he asked us to return to the recruiting station to talk about jobs. I scored the highest in the administrative field and my brother scored highest for motor transport. Both jobs sounded good to us and now the recruiter asked how soon we wanted to leave for boot camp. I wanted to leave immediately but my brother had to wait a month until school was out for the summer.

That next Saturday we spent the day at the Richmond Military Entrance Processing Station (MEPS) taking a physical, followed by the oath of enlistment. We agreed to enlist on the Buddy Program, which meant that we would be assigned to the same platoon throughout boot camp. We also agreed to leave on May 25, 1981. I really felt good about the whole ordeal. Now my parents didn't have to bear the burden of draining their bank account and I could start another episode of my life. The next hurdle to negotiate was to inform my parents that I was dropping out of school and enlisting in the Corps.

After a few days, I called my parents to let them know what had transpired. I could detect the disappointment in their voices but I assured them that I would still get my degree and that the Corps would pay for it. They were really looking forward to me being the first in the family to graduate from college. After the initial shock, I truly think that they were excited about my decision. This would benefit them financially and would give me the opportunity to get out on my own and serve my country, just as my father did, but with the Few and the Proud, the Marines.

Chapter Two

CROSSING THE BURNING SANDS OF PARRIS ISLAND

My brother and I departed from the train station in Richmond, Virginia for boot camp at Parris Island, South Carolina on May 26, 1981. There were about six of us who left from Richmond. One young lady had also taken the challenge to become a U. S. Marine. It was about an eleven hour trip to Charleston because the train stopped many times along the way. It was hard not to think about the videos we had seen at the recruiting station. I visualized drill instructors yelling every time they saw us move.

The time really didn't bother us because we knew that it would be our last chance of freedom for three months. We amused ourselves by joking the entire trip until we arrived to Charleston. There we got our first taste of what it was going to be like trying to become a Marine. When our train stopped, we stepped off and were greeted by a Corporal who immediately started yelling at us to line up single file and to follow him. He led us outside where he attempted to intimidate us by threatening to punch us if we didn't follow orders. He actually punched one of the youngsters that made the trip with us. This came as a shock to the guys we were with because this was something that they weren't expecting. Since my brother and I pledged a fraternity in college this was something that we could relate to and we knew that it was not going to be worse than pledging. Mentally we played along as if we were scared.

From the train station they herded us onto buses for the last leg of our trip. We still had a forty-five minute ride to Parris Island. The bus was very quiet because we all tried to take advantage of the opportunity to sleep. It was already after midnight and we knew that once there, we weren't going to get much sleep.

We felt the bus decelerate and we knew that we were close to Parris Island. Most of us were wide awake now, looking out of the windows. The anxiety was unbearable. I knew that life would be tough for the next 12 weeks. We passed through the gate and down a long dark road. We couldn't see anything to our left or right; no buildings, cars, or street lights. Our recruiters told us that there was only one way on and off Parris Island, a swamp on both sides.

We finally stopped at a long building and the bus door immediately opened. A drill instructor came aboard the bus and began yelling for us to get on the yellow footprints in the front of the building. It seemed like everyone rushed to the door simultaneously. While we were on the yellow footprints, the drill instructors asked who of us came in on the Buddy Program. If you came in on the Buddy Program, you would be assigned to the same platoon. My brother and I did enlist under the Buddy Program but neither of us wanted to say anything. They then split the group in half and both groups went separate ways. I didn't see my brother again until our seventh week at boot camp.

From there we went to a classroom to start our in-processing. We were given several forms and were told not to start filling them out until told to do so. We were instructed block by block. The fatigue was making it difficult to pay attention because by now it was about 2:30 a.m. and the forms kept coming. Upon completing our in-processing, we were directed to a large room with several bunk beds aligned on each side. We were told in Richmond not to bring any valuables, so none of us had watches. I assumed that it was around 4:00 a.m. when we were finally able to get some sleep.

Before I could sink into a deep sleep, we were awakened by the sound of screaming drill instructors banging on metal trash cans. They told us to get on line, meaning to stand at the end of your bunk (bed) in line with the others so that they can count everyone to see if anyone tried to sneak out overnight. There was no need to make the beds because no one had covers. Prior to leaving for our first breakfast, we were told that we had to eat quickly. Breakfast was horrible and we didn't get the chance to finish it anyway. By the time we sat down and had two forks of potatoes, we were told to get up, grab our trays, and head to the door.

From the chow hall we went to the barber shop. It seemed like everyone got six strokes with the clippers and they were done. The barbers spent about thirty seconds on each head, just as we had seen in the videos at the recruiting station.

From the barber shop we went to clothing to get our uniforms. They made this process simple. You walked by with your basket, yelled out your size, and the workers threw your articles in your basket. We were able to pick our own toiletries like soap, shower shoes, and shaving kits. We were then taken to our living quarters, or "squad bay," which was a long room with bunk beds and wall lockers on each side. We were assigned bunks in alphabetical order and were given a wall locker and a foot locker. This is where all of our possessions were kept. For those that forgot to lock their foot lockers when they left their areas, they often came back to a flipped foot locker with all their possessions sprawled over the center of the squad bay.

We were told by our drill instructors to change our clothes and to get on line. It was now time to meet our Series Commander and drill instructors. They assembled us on the floor sitting with our right hand on our right knee and left hand on our left knee. This is the way we would sit for all of our periods of instructions. Our Series Commander introduced our Drill Instructors and all four took an oath to train us to the best of their abilities. Our Senior Drill Instructor spoke to us and then turned us over to the others. Senior Drill Instructors have been on the drill field for a while and trained us alongside the less experienced drill instructors. We were given all of the rules-what to say and what not to say, what to do and what not to do. They distinctly told us that the swamp on both sides of the only road to Parris Island was filled with alligators. They told us not to try our luck in leaving because we would not make it alive.

That night we were allowed to make a ten second phone call home. We were instructed to tell our parents that we had arrived to Parris Island and that we would be in touch. They also said in a very serious manner that we'll start with 67 recruits but everyone won't make it to graduation. Those who had disciplinary problems or couldn't keep up academically would be recycled, meaning that they would go backwards in training with another platoon that was further behind. This kept them at boot camp longer than the expected three months.

This was the beginning of our first phase of boot camp. I was in Hotel Company, Platoon 3032. We began learning Marine Corps customs and courtesies, core values, ethics, first aid, Marine Corps history, and interior guard. Those subjects were combined with physical fitness, running the circuit course, obstacle course, confidence course, pull-ups and sit-ups.

One of the obstacles we encountered during the confidence course was the "Slide for Life." This was two plat-formed towers about 75 yards apart with a rope connecting the two, hanging about ten feet above some murky brown water. The water was only about five feet deep but the drill instructors didn't tell us that. We were under the impression that it was about ten feet deep. The objective of the "Slide for Life" was to climb to the tower platform, lie on the rope, and pull your body across to the other tower. The tricky part was balancing your body on the rope while pulling yourself across. If you lost your balance while negotiating the rope, the drill instructors would tell you to hang from the rope and then drop into the murky water. A week prior to my platoon going to the "Slide for Life," they found a six-foot alligator in the water of the obstacle. They also found another gator walking across the parade deck at First Battalion.

The platoon's uniform for physical training was a t-shirt, a pair of shorts, and running shoes. This made it very easy for the mosquitoes and sand fleas to eat us alive every morning that we came out to do physical training. It's a terrible feeling when you're standing at the position of attention and you feel the mosquitoes and sand fleas biting. You can't move while at the position of attention, and it seemed like the mosquitoes and sand fleas knew it. The drill instructors had to give us permission to slap them. Otherwise, they said that the mosquitoes and sand fleas had to eat too. When they really got bad, our drill instructors would give us the command to "attack" and we would get about ten seconds to slap and scratch. Later during our training, they gave us the remedy for mosquitoes and sand fleas.

The following week we had medical exams, which included check-ups and shots. Eye exams were given also but glasses weren't available for two weeks. Dental exams were the next week. Every day we had a training schedule to follow and our drill instructors kept a copy of the schedule in their smokeys (Drill Instructor hats) that they wore. When it came time to eat, our drill instructors always said that we were having duck. That meant that we would duck in and then duck out. The bottom line was that we get in quickly, and leave quickly. All of the recruits had to wait in line but the drill instructors didn't. When they were through eating, we were too.

After our first week we started receiving mail. My wife, who was my girlfriend then, wrote me about five times a week. I always looked forward to our evening mail call when we received our mail. I wrote her about three times a week.

Discipline is one of the trademarks of the Marine Corps but I took it lightly at boot camp, which meant that I spent a lot of time on the quarter deck. The quarterdeck was where we had to go for physical punishment. Whenever we got into trouble or aggravated our drill instructors, they sent us to the quarterdeck. It was just a little area in the squad bay where they would make us do side straddle hops (jumping jacks), push-ups, bends and thrusts, leg lifts and mountain climbers until we almost vomited. Sometimes we would be there for ten minutes depending on the severity of what we did.

I had a problem of laughing and I was always getting caught. At times I wouldn't be laughing and one particular drill instructor would send me to the quarterdeck anyway. I can hear him saying, "You know where to go, Recruit Camp." I got so immune to the quarterdeck. Sometimes I would end up in a puddle of sweat on the quarterdeck.

I went through boot camp during the hottest months of the summer, May through August. If we were outside, they would send us to the pit. The pit was a large box of sand that served the same purpose of the quarterdeck. Sometimes, the entire platoon would end up in the pit. Sand mixed with sweat is not a good combination, and our shower time did not give us the time to fully clean ourselves. Our shower time was pretty much like the chow hall. We were in and out in no time. Can you imagine 67 Marines in the shower at one time with about five minutes to shower? Needless to say, if you weren't one of the first ones in, you didn't get time to scrub the dirt off.

Field days involved a lot of teamwork and that's one thing that the Corps stressed. Field days were the days we cleaned the squad bay. Cleaning consisted of moving the racks (bunk beds) and footlockers from one side of the squad bay to the other, then sweeping and swabbing (mopping). Then we would do the other side. Different squads were assigned tasks under the watchful eyes of our drill instructors. Two squads cleaned the head (bathroom) and two squads cleaned the portholes (windows and ledges). One squad cleaned the ladder well (stairwell). We were given about forty-five minutes to have this done. Our drill instructors timed us for almost everything we did. When our time was up, they counted from ten to one backwards and then yelled, "Zero." We would then say, "Freeze Recruit, Freeze." Everyone would stop then. Whoever was not finished would automatically go to the quarterdeck. This was especially effective after we woke up and had to put our clothes on. A few were always caught with untied boots or unbuckled belts.

"Square away time" was the time designated in the evenings to spit shine our shoes, read and write letters, or just talk amongst ourselves. We usually had mail call during square away time. That was great because when we received photos of our families, we could share them right then. We also had a board on the wall next to the drill instructor's hut where we could post photos of our wives and girlfriends. I never posted any. Many of our platoon members were joked with about their photos. Later in second and third phases, we would utilize our square away time to prepare our uniforms for inspections and to study our knowledge for our essential subject exam.

The platoon loved to spend time on the parade deck for drill. Drill was another aspect that the Corps emphasized. We could not wait until the point when all of our drill instructor's commands were executed with perfection. We spent a lot of time in the pit because we couldn't master the technique of many of the movements right away. Even if we did well, we would still end up in the pit. It was part of the mental game they played on us.

A special thing about drill was the cadence that was called by some drill instructors. If they called a good cadence, it would really motivate us to do well. Some Drill Instructors even sang the cadence and that would motivate us to no end. We loved to go to the parade deck while the other platoons were practicing drill because this would give us the opportunity to hear the other drill instructors call their cadence. It seemed like each of them had their own original cadence. Back at the chow hall, it was great when we marched by the platoons that had a week or two before graduation. I remember staring at a third phase platoon and reading the lips of one of the recruits saying, "Get your eyeballs off of us." We hadn't gotten to their level of expertise yet. While back at the squad bay, we would often hear each other trying to emulate our drill instructor's cadence. We were evaluated for Initial Drill and we did well although we didn't win the competition within our series. We could redeem ourselves at Final Drill. We had four platoons in our series and we competed for areas like drill, academics, physical fitness, and rifle qualification.

Swim Week looked to be a challenge for many of us. We were told and our drill instructors demonstrated that we could actually float with all of our gear on. When Marines conducted amphibious landings and beach assaults, we did this from ships or landing craft. History has noted that there were occasions where some Marines making assaults from ships drowned because they couldn't swim. Some amphibious watercraft couldn't come into the shore far enough, so that left the Marines to disembark in water over their heads. This was why swim qualification was so important.

The initial part of the swim qualification was easy if you could swim. Those who could not swim were separated from the others and they received special instructions. We were taught how to inflate our camouflage utility uniforms to act as floatation devices, and how they would keep us afloat out in the open water as long as you continued to splash water on them. We were also taught how to pack our backpacks and use them for floatation devices. We actually had to pack them and demonstrate how effective our packing was by swimming 50 meters with our packs on. I was thoroughly convinced that it worked. Swim Week was a great experience but we still had Marines that couldn't swim. They had to get further instructions once they got to the fleet because it was an annual requirement. After Swim Week we had our five mile hike out to the rifle range. This started our Phase II training.

Phase II started at the Rifle Range with Grass Week. Grass Week was where we received marksmanship instructions on how to lay, sit, and stand to shoot the M16A1 rifle. We also received comprehensive instructions on elevation, wind age, sight alignment, sight picture, and breathing. Rifle qualification is one of the most important aspects of becoming a Marine because whatever your Military Occupational Specialty (MOS) was, every Marine was considered an Infantryman or Infantrywoman. Knowing how to shoot saved lives and it was a must on the battle field. We're taught at Grass Week how to lie down and manipulate our rifle slings to get the maximum benefit from our shooting. We're taught how to get into a tight sitting position that allowed our elbows to rest on the inner portions of our feet. We're taught how to raise and lower our rifles in the standing position and squeeze the trigger just as the front sight post enters the black portion of the target. We qualified from 200, 300, and 500 yards, and believe me, at 500 yards, the man-size target looks very small from that distance. They gave us one week of Grass Week, the next week we fired at the targets.

It was very important that we listened on the firing lines. Safety was paramount while on the range. All it took was one accidental round discharge and that would temporarily shut the range down while the range officials investigated. We were given four days of firing before we had to qualify for our rifle badges that we would display on our uniforms for graduation. We could either fire marksman, sharp shooter, or expert. The first two or three days we worked on our elevation and wind age. The extra days were for technique and breathing. We were also given data books to record our weapon's data and shots. The data books really came in handy. We qualified on the fifth day and as a platoon we didn't do to bad. Those that did not qualify had to stay at the range and joined another platoon until they did qualify. While on the range I ran into my fraternity brother who was on mess duty. His platoon was serving the food for us. I didn't get a chance to talk with him but he doubled the food up on my plate. Our next challenges were the Field Week and the eight-mile sustainment hike.

Field Week was fun. It started with finding a bivouac area or place to set up our tents. We immediately began learning tactics and squad movements. When we weren't getting a period of instruction, we were rehearsing our knowledge. We had our academics testing in the next phase. We spent all of one day maneuvering through obstacles as a squad. We were given a few items to utilize while maneuvering. The obstacles required thinking and teamwork. We were monitored closely by a drill instructor who would give us a tip every now and then if we strayed to far off course.

While in the field, we ate MREs, or Meals-Ready-To-Eat. They came in brown pouches and they weren't that bad. There was a wide assortment to choose from but when they were issued, we were told to grab three out of the box and go. We always traded later. Three MREs a day provided enough calories to allow us to stay in a field environment for quite some time. Besides the obstacles, we played war games against the other platoons. Most of the time we were the aggressors attacking them in their fighting holes. We never found out which platoons were victorious.

The last day of Field Week we went to the gas chamber. The gas chamber showed us firsthand if our gas mask worked or not. First we went through classes on how to take the mask apart, how to exchange parts, clean it, and how to clear it from having gas inside. The sole purpose for this exercise was for us to build confidence in our gas mask. While in the chamber with our masks on, they lit cesium (CS) gas capsules and asked if anyone had leaks in their masks. If everyone was alright, they had us do jumping jacks and then shake our heads back and forth to see if we had a tight seal with our mask around our faces. When everyone was alright, they had us pull up our masks and let some CS gas in. Then we had to clear the mask with the technique we learned. If you didn't do the technique properly, you'd breathe in a lot of gas. This caused burning eyes and throats, nausea, and vomiting for those that could not clear their masks. The bad thing is that the drill instructors didn't let them out of the chamber when it happened. Basically, they had to suffer until we all were let out. Some of the drill instructors thought that was amusing to watch. The mask confidence exercise definitely had me confident.

Phase III started once we were back to the squad bay. This is when our drill instructors told us the secret about the mosquitoes and sand fleas. It was Skin-So-Soft by Avon. It worked like a charm and it didn't smell bad. They would let us use it for physical training and inspections. We had our initial uniform fitting scheduled that week. These were the uniforms that we took with us to the fleet. Everything had to fit. The uniforms that didn't fit were sent to tailoring and were returned the next week for our second fitting. We also started our academic review for our comprehensive exam. This exam consisted of everything we had learned since arriving to Parris Island. We didn't have anyone that failed the exam. Final Drill came fast but we were prepared for it. We received a fairly good score but we didn't score high enough to win the drill competition for the series.

Our sustainment hike was our final hike for boot camp. Our goal was to sustain a good pace for the entire ten-mile hike. It was conducted with full pack and gear. The platoon as a whole did well, minus some major blister injuries. Even after we changed boots and put on dry socks, some still suffered with painful blisters. Half way through the hike, we stopped at a large open area with a large set of bleachers. The entire series was seated in the bleachers. There was a disabled tank in the open field about 300 yards away. We were told to stay tuned for the "one million dollar minute." We didn't have the slightest idea of what they were talking about. Two Marines came forward with an M-203 grenade launcher and fired a few grenades at the disabled tank. They registered a couple of hits. Next, a .60 caliber machine gun was brought out and the Marines open fired on the tank. They had target practice with the tank. Tow dragons were next in the assault. They registered two direct hits. A tank rolled in from the left side of the open field and hit the tank with two rounds. Lastly, 2 cobra helicopters appeared over the trees and fired two missiles each at the disabled tank. About one minute later, all of the weapons opened fired at the tank for a full minute. The onslaught of firepower produced a cloud of smoke around the tank. When the smoke cleared the tank was demolished. That was the "one million dollar minute." The price of the ammunition fired by all weapons for one minute, cost about one million dollars. This was a demonstration of the superior fire power of our Marine arsenal. It was very impressive.

Since we had our second uniform fitting, we were then ready for our Company Commander's Inspection that week and our Battalion Commander's Inspection the following week. Both inspections were with our rifles so they took many hours of preparation. Our drill instructors really stressed how important it was to keep our rifles clean. On the battlefield there was nothing more important. One night they even had us sleep with our rifles in our racks (beds) and they made us repeat the "Rifle Creed" over and over. We were required to learn the creed prior to leaving the rifle range and we did.

The Company Commander only inspected about fifteen Marines in the platoon. The others he just walked by. If the Company Commander stopped in front of you, you conducted Inspection Arms with your rifle. He took your rifle and inspected it. Not only did he inspect you and your weapon, but he asked questions from the academic subjects that would appear on our exam. The following week, the Battalion Commander pretty much did the same thing. Our platoon was successful in both inspections.

After the inspection evolutions, we felt a sense of accomplishment that is hard to describe. Those were our last two major hurdles before graduation. The hard part was over and now all we had to do was stay out of trouble and we would proudly walk across that parade deck for graduation. We only had eight days of boot camp left and one of those days we would utilize for base liberty, or a day where we were free of training and we could tour the rest of the base. That Saturday was our Liberty Day. We went anywhere on the base we wanted, ate what we wanted, made phone calls, shopped at the exchange or just hung around the squad bay without the watchful eyes of our drill instructors. Our drill instructors released us at 9:00 a.m. and we didn't have to return until 6:00 p.m. Of course we had a threatening lecture before we left the squad bay. We were given all of the liberty rules and were told that anyone who broke the rules, would be dealt with accordingly. The first place I went to was the snack bar to eat. I hadn't had a soda since I left Richmond, Virginia for boot camp. Eleven weeks is a long time to wait to quench your thirst. Liberty was a blast and everyone stayed out of trouble. By this time we all started to get a little cocky. We realized that unless we had a major discipline issue, we would all graduate with the platoon. Our drill instructors sensed it but still reinforced the point that we hadn't graduated yet and that they were waiting to make an example out of someone.

The following Monday we started graduation rehearsal. I called my parents to see if they would be making the trip down to Parris Island for my graduation. They were coming down and bringing my girlfriend along with them. I was elated to hear that my girlfriend would be in attendance. That was really motivating. My father said that they would arrive that Thursday, the day before graduation. We practiced for graduation Monday through Wednesday morning. The afternoons were utilized for administrative matters such as getting orders to our next duty stations and flight reservations. I, like several of my platoon mates, had orders to Camp Lejeune. I was headed to Third Battalion, Sixth Marines and I didn't know anything about the unit. I knew that Camp Lejeune was a large base and from our history classes, it was named after a famous general, John A. Lejeune. Thursday was our five mile motivation run or MOTO run. We ran a totally different route around the base. We passed by many spectators but I never saw my family. After the MOTO run we packed and traded addresses and phone numbers. We were in our racks that night but we didn't get much sleep. We were all anxious for graduation. You could wake up and hear recruits whispering. Any other time, all you heard was snoring.

Friday finally came and this was our day. This was the final day of our twelve week initiation into the world's most famous fighting force. We marched to the chow hall that morning with an extra sense of pride and accomplishment, as the newly formed platoons stared at us with envy. They too knew that we were graduating and the looks on their faces told it all. When we returned to the squad bay, we staged our gear outside. That way, after graduation we could just grab and go. Graduation was at 10:00 a.m. but our drill instructors wanted us in place at 9:15 a.m. As we marched up to the Parade Deck, we could see the families anxious to catch a glimpse of their new Marines. We could see them pointing and smiling as we marched into position. The graduation lasted about forty-five minutes. We were dismissed and immediately ran into the crowd to look for our families. It really felt good to see them and I thanked them for driving down from Virginia to see me graduate. I recall thinking to myself as they played the Marine Corps Hymn, we had now claimed the title of United States Marines. We were a part of a legacy that has fought successfully in all of our nation's major conflicts. We've earned the recognition of Devil Dogs as given to us by the Germans because of the tenacious way we fought in the Battle of Belleau Woods. I realized then why only the Marines guard our nation's Embassies abroad. There was no other branch of service that had the discipline and war fighting spirit that Marines possessed. We were now, the Few, the Proud, the Marines and we had crossed the burning sands of Parris Island.

Chapter Three

THE DOORWAY TO PARADISE

When most people think about Hawaii, they automatically associate it with paradise. Islamically, relating to the title of this chapter, I'm speaking of paradise in a greater sense. This paradise can only be obtained by submitting to do the will of Allah (swt), and enjoining all that is good and forbidding all that is evil. This paradise is the paradise that is vividly described in the Quran. This paradise is the final resting place of your soul for those whose scale was heavy on the side of good deeds and actions, and we received Allah's (swt) favor to enter the pearly gates. It was in Hawaii where I was introduced to Islam, that which we consider the Doorway to Paradise.

Growing up Baptist left a spiritual void in my life. Although my parents kept us involved in various church activities, such as the choir, the usher board, and Bible School, my siblings and I didn't have a clue as to why we even went to church. Our thought was that we were attending because everyone else was attending and that it was the thing to do. I can probably say that it was the very same way when my parents were growing up. No one sat us down and explained any Christian concepts to us like the Trinity, Baptismals, the Holy Ghost or any of the other concepts that were affiliated with the church. Basically, the church was a place where we went to see our friends and family once a week and around Easter we went shopping for new clothes to wear on Easter Sunday. I recall how my brothers and I would lie in the bed on Sunday morning with our door closed, hoping that our father wouldn't knock on it and say, "Time to get up for church." We would then mumble under our breath so that my father didn't hear us. Sometimes he wouldn't come to our room and we would lie in bed until we heard them leave for church, and then we would get up venture throughout the neighborhood.

As I grew older and was able to understand what went on in the church, I started to question the things that I couldn't come into terms with. For example, if your pastor was an engineer working at the N.A.S.A. Space Center, why was the church paying him such a large salary? I recall that Jesus (Pbuh) preached the Gospel for three and a half years and never asked for a dime. Jesus (Pbuh) was strictly focused on saving people's souls. Preachers in the pulpit were more concerned about lining their pockets with dollars, and they were telling their congregations that God wanted them to wear $400-$500 suits and $300 shoes; to build mansions and drive expensive cars. To make matters even worse, some of them were the worst hypocrites in the church. I could tell the effectiveness of the pastor by the words and actions of the congregation. We had issues in our church that were associated with the choir, the deacons, the pastor and many followers in the congregation. The same issues were prevalent in just about all of our local churches. I really had a problem with that and it couldn't have been considered good Christian behavior. We referred to it as "playing church." When I talk with friends and family today, they tell me that the same issues are prevalent in the church now as they were when I was growing up. Their focus was not on God. Too many of their followers were concerned about who's wearing what, what kind of car they drove, and what size their house was.

I asked why that if the Bible stated in Deuteronomy and Leviticus not to eat pork and not to even touch it, why did Christians eat it? You would not believe some of the answers they would give to justify why they ate it. The worst explanation that I heard was that in the days of the Prophets, they didn't have refrigerators to keep the pork safe to eat. Today we have refrigerators to keep it from going bad, so the Lord said that it was permissible to eat. I found it strange that the Muslims and the Jewish didn't eat pork but Christians did. Wasn't Jesus (Pbuh) a Hebrew? I also found it strange that with all of the scriptures read in church by the pastors, I've never heard the two read about not eating or touching pork.

To this day, no Christian has been able to explain the Trinity to me in a way that makes sense. The Trinity is the foundation of the Christian faith and is referred to as the Father, Son, and Holy Ghost but yet, the Revised Standard Version of the Bible now reads the 1st Epistle of John 5:7 as:

"And the spirit is the witness, because the spirit is the truth. There are three witnesses, the spirit, the water, and the blood; and these three agree."

The RSV even goes on to say that "although the King James Version of the Bible has with good reason been termed the Noblest Monument of English Prose, it still has grave defects." It further stated that "these defects are so many, and so serious, as to call for revision of the English translation."

In addition to nullifying the Trinity, there were also verses in the Bible that refuted the concept of Jesus (Pbuh) being God, and verses that actually referred to Jesus (Pbuh) as a prophet.

The fact really boggled my mind of how Jesus (Pbuh) went from messenger of God, how the Muslims see him, to son of God, and then to God himself, and nobody questioned that concept. While Jesus (Pbuh) was on the cross in Matthew 27:46, he cried out:

"My God, my God, why hast thou forsaken me?"

Who was Jesus (Pbuh) crying out to? This clearly illustrated that Jesus (Pbuh) was crying out to God and not himself. God does not need to cry out for anyone or anything.

On another note, the Muslims recognized Jesus (Pbuh) as a prophet of God and the Bible verified this. Read Matthew 21:11 and Luke 24:19.

"and the crowds said, this is the prophet Jesus (Pbuh) from Nazareth of Galilee."

"and they said to him, concerning Jesus (Pbuh) of Nazareth, who was a prophet mighty in deed and word before God and all the people . . ."

These were just two of the many concepts that we were taught growing up in the church. The Quran supported both of the facts that Jesus (Pbuh) was not God, and that he was a prophet. Why were these concepts even in question when both the Christian and Muslim doctrines verified them?

There were so many inconsistencies with the Christian faith and as I ventured from church to church, I noticed the same pattern in each, but some worse than others. After arriving in Hawaii in 1992, I was determined to find a place of worship where my family and I could be spiritually fulfilled and not caught up in the hypocrisy that we had been so accustomed to in our previous churches.

My wife and I began at our Chapel on Kaneohe Bay until we were invited to Kailua Baptist Church by some friends. Neither was what we were looking for so we searched on. We had a cousin and some friends at Pearl Harbor and Hickam Air Force Base so we took a recommendation from them to attend the Chapel at Hickam. They definitely had a family atmosphere so we decided to attend regularly to see if the services would fill our spiritual void. After a couple months of observance, we realized that they provided the same "no business preaching" but we decided to stay there because they had a good choir. In addition, when we made the trip across island, we could always stop by and have dinner with the relatives.

In January of 1994, a good friend of mine approached me and mentioned that there was an Islamic minister coming to the island for a lecture. I had heard about the minister and had seen him briefly on the news. He seemed somewhat controversial on the news and I was curious to know why. I didn't attend his lecture but my friend did. When I talked with him the day after the lecture, he excitedly told me about some of the topics that the minister talked about. He spoke about Black awareness and learning our African American history. He talked about the Muslim slaves coming to the United States from Senegal and the Ivory Coast. He talked about our African presence in Egypt, Europe, and Asia and about cleaning up black neighborhoods in our cities from drugs and prostitution. From what I had seen on television, his organization was doing just that. They were actually cleaning up black neighborhoods from New York, to Chicago, to California. He discussed black men taking responsibility for their families and raising children properly. He also talked about women dressing properly and carrying themselves with pride and dignity. After I heard that, I thought back to my college days when the Muslim female basketball player wore sweat pants when she played. Now I fully understood why she dressed the way she did. He concluded with how blacks should start their own businesses, make jobs for other blacks and stop looking for handouts from the government. He didn't touch on anything spiritual but the other topics made a lot of sense to me.

All of these topics peaked my interest and I started asking myself if this was what I had heard at the numerous churches I had attended. My friend also mentioned that they had started an Islamic study group in Waipahu and that they met every Sunday. I began to do some research on Islam, and I was excited to attend the study group that coming Sunday.

The more I thought about becoming Muslim, the more I thought about how my immediate and extended family would react to it. I would be the first Muslim in two generations of family that I knew of and I was concerned that I would no longer be accepted in the family because of my new found way of life. We did have cousins in New Jersey with Muslim names but I don't know if they were practicing Muslims. Was accepting Islam worth breaking family tradition? I really did believe so, especially after experiencing some of the issues my family had experienced as Christians. I asked myself if my family would've been any different if we were raised as Muslims. The foundation and principles of Islam were a lot more logical and there was nothing confusing about the doctrine. Historically, it was a fact that some of the slaves that came from Senegal and the Ivory Coast were Muslims. Regardless of whose history books you read, you can't refute that. Another question that I had to ask myself was do I continue to be a Christian because my parents were Christians? That really seemed to be the case in our society. This was a critical decision and one that would decide the fate of my soul come Judgment day.

It was at that point when I told my wife that I was contemplating becoming a Muslim. She didn't display any reaction but she asked me if I was going to have four wives. That was usually the only thing that Christian women knew about Islam. I assured her that she didn't have to worry about me having four wives. I broke the news to my mother also and she did have a reaction. Very displeased with me, she told me that the organization was a cult and that she didn't want anything else to do with me. I felt bad but what could I say? For someone that never taught us anything about Christianity, I couldn't understand why she felt that way. I was really hurt but I decided to leave the situation alone and let time heal it. About a month later, I recall hearing my wife tell my mother on the phone that many of my old bad habits, I didn't do any more. It was at that time when she wouldn't even speak to me on the phone. After a few months, we started to communicate again. My father never said anything either way. He was always laid back and never said too much. Neither my brothers nor sister ever said anything about my reversion to Islam. I say reversion because Muslims believe that everyone is born submitting to do the will of God, which is the definition of a Muslim. It's their parents that change them to Christian, Buddhist, or any other faith. So instead of converting to Islam, I reverted to Islam.

After I became Muslim, I picked up one of the habits from the brothers. When I answered the telephone, I would answer, "As Salaam Alaikum," (Peace be unto you). My wife really got angry when she heard me say this until one day I asked her if she knew what it meant. She replied "No." I explained to her what it meant and showed her throughout the New Testament where Jesus (Pbuh) said "Peace be unto you." She replied that "Jesus (Pbuh) didn't say it like that." I told her that Jesus (Pbuh) spoke Hebrew and Aramaic, so he didn't say it in English. After the explanation, it was alright for me to answer the phone in that manner.

There were four of us that drove from Kaneohe Bay that Sunday. We met with a group of Army military members and about four civilians. The study group started off with us all standing for the prayer and then reading from a study guide. The study guide contained facts about how far the earth was from the sun, the earth from the moon and so on. I couldn't understand what these facts had to do with the religion. We didn't read any Quran and I was glad because I didn't have one. Later I asked the brother where I could get one. He told me that there was a black owned bookstore in Pearl City called Black Imani that sold them. I picked one up that next Saturday.

For the next few weeks the study group went through the same routine. From what I had read about Islam, the Quran was the focal point of the religion. The group never seemed to get to the Quran so I asked why we never read it. The brother responded by telling me that the minister wanted all of the study groups to focus on the study guides. When we finally started reading the Quran, I noticed that a couple of brothers used a different translation of the Quran from the one we read. When I asked what the difference was, I was told that the one we read, the Maulauna Muhammad Ali translation, was the one that the minister used. The other two brothers used the Abdullah Yusuf Ali translation. I later found out that although the translations are different to some extent, the Arabic was exactly the same and that the Maulauna Muhammad Ali translation was not that good. In fact, it was the worst translation from Arabic to English of all of the most popular Qurans.

As I read the Quran on my own, I started to notice contradictions in what was being taught by the Study Group and what was in the Quran. For instance, the Quran said to fast during the month of Ramadan, the 10th month of the lunar calendar, but we were being taught to fast during the month of December around Christmas time. I read in a book of Hadith, which are things the Prophet Muhammad (Pbuh) said and did, that Muslim men shouldn't wear gold, but every time we saw the minister on video he had gold jewelry on. The Hadith also stated that the Prophet Muhammad (Pbuh) said for us to pray as we saw him pray, bowing and prostrating, but we were being taught not to pray like the Arabs.

There were many more contradictions and I kept notes of what I was learning about Islam in my research and what was being taught at the study group. One particular issue that I had a problem with about the study group was that race was always a topic of discussion, and that was contrary to what I was learning from my research about Islam, the Quran and the Hadith. I remember asking why we didn't have any white members in the organization. I was told that we had to focus ourselves before we let any whites in. That seemed a bit strange to me because I had seen documentaries on television and in my research that there were millions of white Muslims. Something didn't click here, and it wasn't until I saw the movie Malcolm X that the light finally came on. Since he was the leader of this group at one time, I figured that I could get a good perspective of the organization through his portrayal in the movie.

The movie did just that, and then I realized why there were no whites in the organization. The organization was a Black Nationalist group with racist views against whites and the Jewish. This was something that I wasn't used to. With all of my close white friends and a Jewish friend from my first duty station, I could not see myself accepting that as a productive form of behavior nor religious doctrine. Even after he went to Mecca and ate and drank from the same utensils as white Muslims, the organization held steadily to their views. He left that organization after he returned from Mecca and started another that was void of that way of thinking. I really knew then that there was something wrong with their form of Islam and I slowly drifted away from the study group.

I started attending the masjid in downtown Waikiki on Fridays where they practiced Al-Islam or The-Islam. It was the only masjid on the island and was always crowded. If you arrived late, you had to pray outside. The masjid was a house that had been gutted out except for a few rooms. The sisters had a smaller house in the back yard. It was totally different from what I was used to with the study group. They prayed differently and they had whites attending. They even talked about spiritual issues that I found intriguing. This was the true side of Islam that I was looking for. I didn't know how to do the prayer so I grabbed a couple of prayer brochures and made it a priority to learn it. Until then I just followed what I saw everyone else doing. The brochure stated that we had to recite Al-Fatihah (the opening part of the Quran) in every prayer. Al-Fatihah is the first chapter or surah of the Quran and it was recommended that you recite it in Arabic. I recall a part in the movie where he was praying in a masjid in Saudi Arabia reciting Al-Fatihah. As he recited it in Arabic in the movie, the words scrolled across the bottom of the screen. I kept rewinding the movie until I learned Al-Fatihah.

Shortly after I started attending the masjid, my unit began preparing for a six-month deployment to Okinawa. I was serious about Al-Islam and I didn't want to leave the masjid not knowing what Okinawa had to offer in the area of Islamic services. I couldn't avoid the deployment so I took all of my books and study material to keep me occupied while in the absence of Muslims.

We arrived in Okinawa in June of 1995. The day after arrival we attended our Welcome Aboard Brief where the island organizations and services explained what they had to offer for island personnel. The Chaplain from Marine Corps Bases, Japan was there and he announced that there were Islamic services offered on Fridays at 1:15 p.m. Once my unit was settled into our new home, I made my way to service that next Friday.

I caught the base shuttle bus to the Chapel at Camp Foster. The Muslim Prayer Room (musallah) was located upstairs on the catwalk of the chapel. It was a small room and with the book shelves in, we hardly had enough room to do the prayers when more than seven Muslims attended. Once we had consistent numbers attending Friday service, the chapel gave us the nursery next door that had a lot more space. We then used the old musallah as a library. One of the Air Force brothers was the Islamic Lay Leader and he served as the Imam. On a good day we would have between six to ten brothers show up. I saw that they prayed like the Muslims at the Masjid in Hawaii so I assumed that they were Sunni Muslims. We talked after the prayer. I told them what I had experienced with the study group and a few of them could relate to what I was saying. They had gone through the same thing. They made sure that I knew the differences between the two ideologies and gave examples of what to look for when talking to those who followed the wrong ideology. I told them that I was learning the prayer and a couple of them were learning it also. They were a good group of Muslims, dedicated to doing the will of Allah (swt) and following the Sunnah (Way) of the Prophet Muhammad (Pbuh).

I tried to attend Jummah every Friday until my unit left for Camp Fuji on Mainland, Japan. The Marines went to Camp Fuji for large scale training. Okinawa was very small so the training sites had limited space. Three months out of our six-month deployment cycle was spent at Camp Fuji. There was not much to do on the Camp so I had ample opportunity to learn the prayer. I brought my Walkman and prayer guide and learned it in about a week; first in English, then in Arabic. I also learned the different positions and movements of the prayer and I couldn't wait to get back to Okinawa to actually do the prayer in congregation with the others and actually know what I was doing. When I returned to Okinawa, I fell right into place with the others.

When I had questions about the prayer and I wasn't with the brothers, I would go down the hall and ask one of the Marines in my unit who was no longer a practicing Muslim. I met him at my unit prior to deploying after I spotted his Muslim name on an alpha roster. I saw him in the hall one day and asked if he was a Muslim. He replied, "Yes, but I'm not practicing." I never asked why. He was very intelligent and extremely knowledgeable about Islam. He was a Muslim prior to the Gulf War in Iraq. He was assigned to working with the Iraqi Prisoners of War, and he built some good relationships with some of the prisoners. Those relationships paid dividends with the Iraqis because he prevented the POWs from eating the pork Meals-Ready-to-Eat (MREs) that the Americans would give them, knowing that eating pork was prohibited in Islam. This upset some of the Marines but to him as a Muslim it was his duty to do it. It was good having him right down the hall if I had questions.

The Muslim community stayed pretty active. We donated time to maintaining a local orphanage, cleaning up senior citizens homes, and assisting with beach clean-ups. We also participated in our base chapel quarterly clean-ups. I tried to spend as much time as I could down at Camp Foster with the brothers as I was trying to learn as much as possible.

Another thing that I liked about the Muslim community was that during any time of the day, you could drive by the musallah and find someone there either studying or praying. We all had keys in our possession so we could drop by any time. Some of us made it a point to do all five prayers there from time to time. Occasionally on Friday or Saturday nights, we conducted discussions and actually slept in the musallah overnight. This really made the community close.

Because I dedicated so much time to learning about Islam and absorbing so much knowledge from the brothers, our six-month deployment went by very quickly. Before long, my unit was returning to Hawaii. When we returned to Hawaii, I picked up where I left off at the masjid. We had visiting scholars who came from different countries to give lectures on many topics. A lecture on Hajj (Pilgrimage to Mecca) really caught my attention, and at that time I made the intentions to go. With lots of encouragement from those who had already made the Hajj, I set my sights on what it would actually take to make the journey.

At my three year mark in Hawaii, I received orders to transfer. My wife and I had wondered where the Marine Corps would send us next. I had received orders to none other but Okinawa, Japan. Very excited about the orders, I contacted the brothers that I had met during my six-month deployment to let them know that I would now become a permanent member of the Islamic community there. Now I was able to show my family the island that I had grown so fond of while deployed. My family would now be able to experience the wonderful Japanese culture that I had talked about when I returned from the Land of the Rising Sun.

Chapter Four

EXPERIENCING OKINAWA, JAPAN (1996-2002)

My family and I arrived in Okinawa in July of 1996. We flew in during the initial stages of a typhoon. Typhoons were new to the family but I had experienced a couple while deployed to Okinawa on the six-month Unit Deployment Program. The wind of a typhoon can roar pretty loud but there's no need to be concerned about danger because the structures there are built for the strong winds. You hardly heard of houses or buildings being uprooted during typhoons, like those of hurricanes in the states. We listened to those winds for two days while we were confined to quarters as the typhoon roared through Okinawa. We utilized the Hamagawa Lodge as our temporary lodging facility until we were assigned housing. We rode the shuttle bus until we purchased our own transportation. It took us about a month to receive housing, which was a four bedroom place with a lot of children in the neighborhood for our children to interact with.

I was stationed at Marine Corps Air Station, Futenma, what Marines called the Air Wing. I was assigned to the Station Adjutant's office, along with the Adjutant and three Japanese secretaries. It was a wonderful job that offered lots of free time to attend college to pursue my degree. After all, I did promise my parents that I would get my degree at some point in my career. I immediately enrolled with the University of Maryland to start finishing up my curriculum in Business Administration.

My wife registered the children for school and their athletic activities. She also contacted the child care center to see what was required for her to become a home day care provider. She figured that if she worked at the house, she would be at home for the children when they returned from school. Thus far, throughout my career, she had been there to help with their homework and to take them to practice or work.

It was great to be back with the Muslim community there at the base. This was the same community I met while deploying from Hawaii twice. Most of the same brothers and sisters were still there. There were also two Muslim communities that existed off of the base. One community consisted of students who attended the University of the Ryukyus, a Japanese university, in which the majority of the Muslims there were from Bangladesh, Indonesia, Malaysia and some parts of Africa. The university was where we held our celebrations for the Islamic holidays. They even had a musallah or small masjid in the Student Union Building, for Friday prayers, and at times, the five daily prayers. There was also the Okinawa International Center (OIC) that brought in professional students from all over the Middle East, Pakistan, Africa, South America, and Fiji, to learn main frame computers, systems analysis, systems design, multi-media and more. They also had a curriculum of Japanese language classes and culture. Many of these students were Muslims. Most of the students came to the OIC for four to five months and then returned to their countries with a wealth of knowledge.

During my first two weeks on Okinawa, I hadn't gone to the OIC or University but I looked forward to going out to meet the Muslims in both locations. In about a week or so, I got the opportunity to visit the OIC. Three of the military brothers and I decided to visit the OIC to see how many Muslims were there and which countries they were from. One of the brothers had been in Okinawa for quite some time and had been to the OIC several times. It was located about fifteen minutes from the base. When we visited, if we didn't know any Muslims there, we would go to the cafeteria at dinner time. This was where all of the ethnic groups congregated. It was there we met, talked, had dinner and then went to the recreation room, one of the lobbies, or to their rooms for tea and conversation. We walked into the cafeteria and could clearly tell what area the Muslims were in. The Muslim sisters wore the hijab or Islamic head covering and usually they all sat together. We met Muslims from Jordan, Syria, Egypt, Morocco, Saudi Arabia, Malaysia, Maldives, Indonesia, and many countries from the African continent. As they always did, they invited us to eat with them. They would never let the visiting brothers pay for their meals. They each were issued meal cards by the OIC and they charged our meals on their cards. The OIC served halal meats, or Islamically slaughtered meats to cater to the Muslim's dietary restrictions. Their meals always included about three or four dishes with halal meat, either chicken, beef, or lamb.

Over dinner, we conversed about our countries, cultures, Islam, and many other topics. Most astonishing to them was the fact that we were once Christians but reverted to Islam. The Muslim brothers and sisters, along with some of the Christians were curious to know why we decided to become Muslims. We each gave our reasons and most of the Christians could relate to our reasoning, especially the Catholics. Once the cafeteria closed, we went to the lobby and I recall meeting a brother there from Iran who was not at the cafeteria with us. The brothers introduced us and he asked where we were from. I told him that we were American. He then asked, "So you're from the land of Shaitan Ahkbar," meaning, "So you're from the land where Satan is the greatest." I replied, "We're American." I could detect the anti-American sentiment in his voice. He didn't reply but he smiled and walked away. The brothers said that he wasn't too social and it probably had something to do with the fact that he was from Iran. Many Iranians were not fond of Americans, and I knew that prior to meeting him. Iran was a country that screened its media from anything that was good about America. The only media they saw or heard about was negative. From the lobby we went to one of the brother's rooms for tea, and then returned to the lobby to pray because it had more space.

Preparing tea for Arabs is like an art. It seemed like each culture took pride in the way they boiled it, mixed the tea, and poured it. The best tea I have tasted thus far have been Moroccan and Tunisian. The Tunisians even added nuts to theirs. Tea was expected every time we visited the OIC. We usually stayed until 10:00 p.m. when visiting hours were over. The OIC definitely became one of the places we would frequent whenever we had the opportunity. It turned out to be a cultural experience every time that we congregated with the Muslims. I started relationships there back in 1996 that I still hold near and dear to my heart to this day.

Our Biggest Jihad (Struggle)

When most non-Muslims hear the word Jihad, they automatically associate it with a holy war or terrorism. Simply put, Jihad is a struggle and it shouldn't be taken out of context to be affiliated with anything relating to terrorism.

Out of all of the brothers we had in the Muslim community on the base, only one had a Muslim wife. Although we all talked with our wives about Islam, strong religious ties and family prevented them from accepting our way of life. Four of the wives were born Roman Catholic and the others Baptist. We constantly explained the concepts of Islam to them but our efforts were projected to deaf ears. The brothers with non-Muslim wives were frustrated but each of us tried to encourage each other to be patient with our wives. Each of us wanted our families to be on the same religious accord like we had heard of and had seen with our religious counterparts from Muslim countries. They often mentioned how nice it was to pray together and to participate in the various religious activities together. At that point in our lives, the Muslim men celebrated the Islamic holidays without our families and the families celebrated the Christian holidays with their respective congregations. Eventually, the wives and families started to attend our occasions and that was one step that we never thought that they would take. This gave them the opportunity to talk with each other and express how they felt about certain issues relating to Islam.

We learned later that many of their fears revolved around misconceptions about the religion. Once they started communicating, they were able to confirm what were misconceptions or not. From the gatherings they started calling each other with questions and stories that aroused their curiosity. Most of the wives had a problem with covering their hair and adhering to the dress code that Islam required of their women. Most of them were not aware that Christian women had a dress code also but most Christian women didn't follow it. Once this fact hit home, it was easy for them to accept it. We also had to explain why there was a dress code in Islam, for men and women. The concept gradually started to make sense to them and they slowly began to change the way they dressed without the brothers saying anything. They were also under the impression that Muslim women had to walk six paces behind their husbands. This was a total misconception. This just added to the fact that any time that Islam is portrayed in a negative manner, it spreads like wildfire to the masses.

It was brought to our attention later that the biggest factor that kept them from accepting Islam was their families. Each of the wives felt that their families would turn their backs on them. My wife's case was of the contrary. Although her family didn't agree with her reversion, they never expressed their displeasure except for her father who was a deacon in the church. He didn't distance himself from her but whenever the opportunity presented itself he would lecture her about what the Lord said from a Christian perspective. When she developed enough knowledge about Islam, she was able to question many of the Christian concepts that he discussed with her, which led to uncertainty in her father's mind about what he had been taught as a child. When the discussions got the point where he couldn't justify or prove his concepts, he would leave her with the famous Christian quote, "You just have to have faith in it." My wife refused to accept that.

Of the Muslim men from that same community that I'm still in contact with, three of us now have Muslim wives. One brother actually divorced his Christian wife for a Muslim sister from Malaysia. Because of his reversion, she took a trip home to the states and didn't return. Unfortunately, he had to resort to that. Family life was so much better after my wife reverted to Islam. We developed a closer relationship and we were able to grow spiritually together and no longer in separate directions. That led to more lectures to the children about Islam and explaining the similarities and differences between the two religions. Once they had a good understanding of the Five Pillars, the Articles of Faith, and what was required of Muslims, then we left it up to them to decide whether or not to accept the faith. The Holy Quran revealed to us that there was no compulsion in Islam and we realized that if we forced them to become Muslim, we would be disobeying the word of Allah (swt). Furthermore, we realized that if we forced them to be Muslim, more than likely they wouldn't be good Muslims. It was then left in His hands to touch their hearts with the desire to become Muslims. One of my children accepted Islam along with my wife after I returned from Hajj, another a year later, and the other two still hadn't accepted Islam. That has led to many discussions with Muslims and non-Muslims because they thought that since we the parents were Muslims, the entire family should've been Muslims. Our Muslim brothers and sisters understood that it's up to the children to accept Islam while our Christian friends felt that the children should accept whatever faith their parents are, much like it had been done for decades. Today's generations of Christians are starting to shun away from that mentality and they're breaking the traditions that were instilled upon them by their parents, and their parent's parents. I see this and I hear it in conversations on a weekly basis with the number of people who are accepting Islam as their way of life.

Crossing the Burning Sands of Mecca

It was every Muslim's dream and obligation to make Hajj, or the pilgrimage to Mecca. This was a life-time goal and all praise is to Allah (swt) that through a miracle in 1999, I was blessed enough to take the journey. In 1998, two brothers from our military community made the pilgrimage through the Military Hajj Program. The military made arrangements with the Saudi government to process Hajj visas and they provided military flights into Bahrain, which was only a bus ride from the Holy City of Mecca. When the two returned from Hajj, they told us about the experience and how it really changed their lives. We sat in a circle at the masjid and asked questions every time that we had the opportunity to do so. These conversations excited everyone about making the pilgrimage. It was at that time when I and another one of the brothers made the intentions to make Hajj the following year. I talked it over with my wife and we started setting money aside to defray the cost of the trip.

Prior to starting preparations for making Hajj, there was something that I had to do that I thought would make my pilgrimage more complete. I wanted to change my name to a Muslim name. I talked it over with my wife and decided on a name that would fit my character and personality. I decided on Hafiz Naim for preserver of tranquility, and Ali after one of the most charismatic boxers and figures of the Muslim world. In Islam it's mandatory to keep your father's last name, so I held on to Camp. My next task was to go to legal to conduct a common law name change to make it legal. One of the military lawyers at the Kadena Legal Services Center drafted the document after asking why I desired to change my name. I simply told him that I was a Muslim and desired to have a Muslim name. He also had to ask if I was changing my name to avoid bill collectors. I replied no, and he signed and notarized the document. The next day I went to my administration office and had the change entered into my military records. I also wrote my creditors and the Social Security Administration so that they too could change my records. Next was my passport. I had just received a brand new passport but it reflected my old name. I went to the American Consulate in Naha and presented my document for the name change. It took about thirty minutes to research it and type an amendment in my passport that read "Also Known as Hafiz Naim Ali Camp." Then I really felt like a Muslim.

After my passport was amended, I notified my sponsor in Saudi Arabia to let him know that we were coming to make Hajj. He told me while he was in Okinawa that if I ever wanted to make Hajj, to let him know. He and his wife attended Ryukyu University in Okinawa, received their degrees and returned home to Saudi Arabia. He majored in Marine Biology and she became a doctor. He was of Indonesian descent but his parents moved to Mecca when he was a small child. His family received their Saudi citizenships many years ago. His wife was born and raised in Saudi Arabia and they had three small children that were born in Okinawa, while they attended the university.

About two months prior to Hajj, I took a trip to Tokyo to visit the Saudi Embassy in order to obtain the Hajj paperwork necessary for the trip. There I met a wonderful brother from Sudan that was extremely helpful in explaining the process. He also told me that if there was anything I needed in order to make the pilgrimage to let him know. When I returned to Okinawa, I immediately began to review the checklist to make sure that everything was accomplished. I called the brother that would make the trip with me about every three days to see if he was making progress. The most important items on the checklist were the shots, the Hajj Visa, and the Hajj expense that had to be paid in Riyals, which is the Saudi Arabian currency. At work the following Monday, I submitted my paperwork requesting permission from my Commander to go to Saudi Arabia for the Pilgrimage. My command had no problem with it at all; in fact they encouraged it.

About a week prior to our departure, we started our final check to see if we had everything. The only item we were missing was the Saudi currency, and we went to one of the local Japanese banks to obtain it. Once in the bank, we were told that they didn't do currency exchanges for riyals and that we had to go to Mainland, Japan to have this done. This news came at a critical time because we only had a week before leaving for Hajj. This meant that we had to book flights to Tokyo and visit a bank there to do the currency exchange. Now we had to utilize more leave and spend more money on another airline ticket, which we wanted to avoid. We were faced with a dilemma that we had to call correctly or else risk the trip to Mecca. We had already purchased our airline tickets, so time was of the essence.

While talking about the dilemma to brothers in the community, one of them revealed that he was leaving for Tokyo in a couple of days to see his relatives before heading stateside to his home of record. He was being discharged from the Marine Corps. He offered to exchange the money at the bank and to take it to the Saudi Embassy to get the Hajj Visas. Then, the good brother at the embassy would FedEx the visas to us before our departure date. This opportunity couldn't have come at a better time and we saw this as a miracle from Allah (swt) to allow us to make the pilgrimage. On the day prior to departure, we received the Hajj Visas and we were set to make our journey to the Holy Land.

The next day we departed Naha for a two hour layover in Taipei and then a day and a half layover in Kuala Lumpur, Malaysia before arriving in Jeddah, Saudi Arabia. A good friend of mine, who was stationed with me at Futenma in Okinawa, had gone to Marine Security Guard School (MSG) a year ago and was now the Detachment Commander at the U. S. Embassy in Kuala Lumpur. He stopped by the command after he finished the school while coming back to pick up his family. He told me that if I ever came to Kuala Lumpur, to give him a call and he would do whatever he could to help me. I called him two weeks prior to inform him about our trip and he offered to pick us up from the airport. He also said that we could stay at his house on the Embassy compound and that we would have full access to his two drivers.

When we boarded for our Malaysia flight on Malaysian Airlines, we noticed that the plane had a small vacant area covered by a pull-curtain. We asked the flight attendant what it was used for. She said that most Malaysians were Muslims and that this was the area that they could pray during flights. The area even showed which way the Qiblah was, or the direction to Mecca. She asked if we were Muslims and we told her yes and that we were going to Hajj. During our entire flight we asked her questions about Malaysian foods, the people, and the culture. By the time our flight ended, we had a pretty good idea of what to expect while visiting.

After arriving at the Kuala Lumpur Airport, we had to pass through immigrations. We immediately noticed our beautiful sisters wearing the hijab or head coverings. One of the sisters noticed my name while stamping my passport and asked if I was Muslim. I replied, "Yes," and greeted her with "As Salaam Alaikum." She returned my greeting and asked what brought me to Malaysia. I told her that we were passing through on our way to Hajj. That definitely excited her and she stated "May Allah (swt) accept your Hajj."

Once out of the airport we noticed a string of white Mercedes Benzes. We were both shocked because these were taxi cabs. We sat down while waiting for my friend and his driver to pick us up. They showed up in no time and we were off to the Embassy compound. It took us about thirty minutes to get to the compound and once inside the gates, we were just down the street from his house. He had one of the largest houses in the compound that housed most of the Embassy civilian staff. It was just he, his wife, the two children and the maid that lived there, so there was more than enough space to accommodate us. We went in and met the family, which I hadn't seen in about a year. That evening we toured Kuala Lumpur and they took us out to dinner. Food was very cheap in Malaysia. We fed seven people with a complete meal of meat, rice, bread, and drinks for $17.

The next morning my brother and I got up early to attend the Fajr prayer at the masjid. We walked to the same masjid that my friend had pointed out to us the night prior. After the morning prayer, we returned to the compound to get more rest and then breakfast. Our flight to Jeddah was a day away, so we had time to sight-see and shop that day. My friend instructed one of the drivers to take us anywhere we wanted to go. We started at the K.L.C.C. Mall and then to another popular spot, Ampang Point. Next we ventured to Little India and Chinatown for the ultimate bargains. It was a must to see the Petronas Towers because they are one of the main attractions of Malaysia. We spent most of the day enjoying the culture and hospitality of the people around the city. We were truly amazed by some of the sights we saw, particularly a family of four that rode on one moped and dodged in and out of traffic with ease. We returned to the compound that evening with a great deal of respect for the Malaysian people and how well the indigenous Malays, the Chinese, and the Indians all lived so well in harmony. We were also thrilled that we could hear the adhan, or call to prayer five times a day and the fact that there was always a masjid close by for prayer. That night we rested for our trip for Hajj the following day.

We arrived in Jeddah early afternoon and started our Hajj processing. All Muslims making the pilgrimage from countries other than Saudi Arabia must go through the Hajj processing in Jeddah, regardless of whether they come by plane, ship, bus or car. This way, the Saudi government can keep track of who comes and leaves the country. We were told during our processing that we wouldn't get possession of our passports again until it was time to leave the country. The first Muslims that we met and talked with in Jeddah were Bosnians. I noticed that they were all white and ranged in age from fifty to seventy years old. We were told that in the geographical area of the world where they come from, most of the inhabitants were white. The Bosnians also told us that their country, just like every other country except America, has a quota of how many pilgrims they can send to Hajj each year. Bosnia sends their senior citizens because they feel that their young Muslims had plenty time left in their lives to go. They went on to tell us that Bosnia received their Islamic influence from the Ottoman Turks who ruled most of that geographical area back in the thirteenth century. That was our first experience of Hajj and we knew that the rest of the time spent in the country was going to be just as interesting.

After our processing, I looked for a pay phone so that I could make a call. My sponsor told me to call his brother for further instructions. I called and he instructed us to go to the city of Madinah in order to do forty prayers in the Prophet Muhammad's (Pbuh) Masjid. This is eight days with five prayers a day at his masjid. This was not part of the actual Hajj but it was customary to do so if you went to Madinah prior to Mecca for Hajj. There were buses that were leaving every fifteen minutes for Madinah and there was no cost involved. The expenses for transportation were covered in our Hajj expenses we paid through the Saudi Embassy prior to our departure from Japan.

We boarded with a busload of pilgrims from West Africa, but I have forgotten what country they were from. A couple of them could speak a little English, so we tried to communicate to the rest through those two. Needless to say, it was an interesting four hour ride to Madinah. When we arrived in Madinah, we stopped at the Hajj office so that they could store our passports. We would have to pick them up prior to leaving for Mecca.

The first thing we had to do in Madinah was to find a hotel for eight days. We had a Sudanese taxi driver take us to an inexpensive hotel and we went inside to make arrangements. It wasn't the best of hotels but it had hot and cold running water and it was just down the street from the Prophet's Masjid (Pbuh). We dropped our backpacks and went out to tour our surroundings. In order to travel as light as possible, we left our luggage at my friend's place in Kuala Lumpur. During the Hajj we would only wear two pieces of white cloth and unstitched slippers or sandals. The two white pieces were called an ihram. This symbolized the simplicity of the pilgrimage. All men making the Pilgrimage must wear the ihram. You could be standing next to the Sultan of Brunei or the King of Saudi Arabia, and you wouldn't even know it.

The Prophet Muhammad's (Pbuh) Masjid was about a quarter-mile from the hotel and you could buy anything in that quarter-mile stretch. The hottest items selling were gold, Quranic compact disks, clothing and prayer rugs. We retired early that night so that we could get a fresh start on our forty prayers the next morning.

We were awaken by the call to prayer (adhan) early the next morning, so we washed up and started our walk down to the masjid. There were thousands of other people heading there also. We were astonished at the size of the masjid. It must have been about a five blocks long and a tall fence surrounded the entire structure. The entire walk-way leading to the masjid on all sides was white marble, and when the masjid was filled to capacity, this was where you had to pray. The Prophet Muhammad's (Pbuh) Masjid was the second largest in the Muslim world behind Al-Masjid Al-Haram in Mecca. We entered the enormous front door where they had guards checking bags for cameras and video recorders. Many Muslims try to take photos and videos inside the masjid but it is strictly prohibited. The guards confiscated them if they were in your possession. Inside the masjid, there was beautiful wall to wall carpet throughout, including on the roof. It was much too hot to pray on the roof in the day time but the evenings are great. The open air allowed germs to escape, unlike the inside where you had to be cautious about coughing and sneezing in closed areas. Every Muslim that I know that has made Hajj has gotten sick at some time during the pilgrimage; we both got sick during our first week on Saudi soil.

Inside the masjid, it was soothing to hear the call-to-prayer echo throughout the structure. I looked forward to getting there early for every prayer so that I could hear it. The masjid even contained the original structure of the Prophet's (Pbuh) Masjid that had been reconstructed several times. Inside that structure were the tombs of the Prophet Muhammad (Pbuh), Abu Bakr, Umar, and Uthman, who were caliphates, or successors of the Prophet Muhammad (Pbuh). There was an empty tomb there for Prophet Isa, or Jesus (Pbuh) when he returned to take the rightly guided to paradise.

We completed our first prayer in the masjid and made our way back to the hotel. We figured that we would go back to sleep, wake up about 10:00 a.m., go for breakfast, and then back to the masjid for the second prayer of the day. We kept the same routine for the entire eight days. The only thing we did different was to venture into different stores on our way to and from the masjid. It was at that time when I called my wife. This was the first time I talked with her since we left Kuala Lumpur. She assured me that everything was alright at home and she informed me that she was reading books about Islam, and was learning. I told her what stage we were in and how things had developed thus far.

We had heard that the Saudi laws for shoplifting were very strict, and it was evident at prayer times. Owners would leave their stores for prayer and would not lock them up. We actually witnessed this ourselves. As soon as the call to prayer was sounded, we saw owner after owner just leave their stores and return after prayer. Some say to cut off one's hand is harsh, but what we learned is that there are a few circumstances that would lead to an offender having their hand amputated. If a person caught stealing was poor and stole to feed his family, he could be spared. To steal for greed could become costly. Needless to say, there was not a lot of shoplifting in Saudi.

Between prayers on our fifth day, we toured the grave sight of the Prophet's (Pbuh) Uncle Hamza and a couple other famous sights in Madinah. I was also able to get my camera to the fence surrounding the masjid to take a few photos of the structure. On the eighth day after we conducted our fortieth prayer in the masjid, we were back to the Hajj office to pick up our passports, and to board the bus for Mecca. The passports were kept in locked bags and we were assured that they were on the bus. The first leg of our Hajj experience was completed.

As we started our journey to Mecca, we were told that the bus would make a few stops on the way. We would stop at the Al-Quba Masjid, a famous landmark, and we would stop at different checkpoints so that the Saudi government could check to see if we all were Muslims. The Saudi government only allowed Muslims into Mecca. If non-Muslims were there, it is for reasons other than Hajj. At every checkpoint, guards would board the bus and ask everyone if they were Muslims. If you looked suspicious they would continue to question you. When we stopped at the Al-Quba Masjid, we were told to purchase the ihram. We put on our ihrams, or two white pieces of cloth and slippers and placed our clothes in our backpacks.

After about two more checkpoints, we entered the city of Mecca. We immediately started looking for the Ka'bah, the first Islamic House of God, built by Abraham and his son Ishmael. As we drove well into the city, we stared through the tall buildings for a glimpse of Al-Masjid Al-Haram which houses the Ka'bah. Suddenly it appeared through the buildings. It was extremely hard to hold back the tears. This was the place that we had heard so much about, and furthermore, it was the house that over one billion Muslims prayed toward when they bow and prostrate five times a day.

After stopping at the Hajj office to relinquish our passports, we were dropped off at a phone because I was instructed to call our sponsor. His parents resided there in Mecca, so when he picked us up, that's where we went. His father met us when we walked in and was very friendly. We caught the aroma of the food as soon as we walked in. His mother had already prepared a meal for us. We sat down and talked with his father for a few minutes and then we washed for prayer and then dinner. We heard his mother talking in the kitchen but we never saw her. When we walked into the dining room, the food was spread out on the floor on top of a table cloth, just as it always was in Okinawa when we visited him and his family at the university. I can't tell you any names of the dishes but everything was good.

For the three days that we stayed with his parents, we prayed at Al-Masjid Al-Haram. We prayed two sunnah rakahs every time we entered the masjid. The structure was extraordinary. The Ka'bah stood in the center of the huge masjid draped in a black cloth lettered with genuine 14k gold Quranic verses. The black stone was visible as well as the door and the guards that guarded it. Twenty-feet from the house stood the Station of Abraham with his footprints inside. About fifty-feet from the house was the stairs that led down into the well of Zam Zam, the same source of water that saved Hagar and Ishmael over fourteen hundred years ago. Surrounding the house on all sides was a pure marble walkway where Muslims could circle the Ka'bah, or as we say, make tawaf.

About seventy-five feet from the house is the location where we enact the running between the As-Safaa and Al-Marwa, the two hills that Hagar ran between searching for water for her and her son Ishmael. The two hills were about one-hundred and fifty yards apart. We could certainly see why this was the largest masjid in the Muslim world. Now we understood why praying one time in this masjid was equivalent to praying 1000 times in any other masjid.

The day prior to the Hajj starting, my sponsor moved us to another house that was owned by another Indonesian family. We stayed with them throughout the Hajj. They had fifteen and ten year old sons, along with two daughters. We never talked with either of their daughters. There was another Indonesian brother staying with them for the Hajj also. He traveled from Mainland, Japan. The three of us stayed in the same room along with their cousin. The next day we embarked on the actual Hajj, the experience of a lifetime.

After putting on our ihrams, we started our Hajj by praying two rakahs in the masjid and then circling the Ka'bah seven times, or making tawaf. We started our tawaf from the corner of the black stone, while saying a supplication. After tawaf, we prayed two rakahs at the Station of Abraham, and then went down to drink some Zam Zam water. Next, we ran between the As-Safaa and Al-Marwah and completed our Umrah, or the lesser Hajj. We returned to the house and looked forward to resuming the Hajj the next day. When we returned to the house, the two sons said that they wanted to take us to a special place. They said that it would take about fifteen minutes to walk there and we were excited to go.

We crossed the highway and began walking through the city. Soon we came to a mountain with a trail of people climbing to its peak. The sons told us that the mountain was called Jabal Al-Nur or Mountain of Light and on the opposite side of the mountain was the cave that the Prophet Muhammad (Pbuh) would go to for meditation. This is also where the

Quran was first revealed to him. We decided to follow the people up to get a look at the famous cave. On our way up, we stopped to take photos with a camel that was being used as a photo prop. You could sit on the camel and get your photo taken for about five riyals or a dollar and fifty cents.

It took us about twenty minutes to get to the cave and the people there were in total chaos. The entrance of the cave was jam packed with people trying to get out and people trying to get in. The entrance of the cave was only about eight-feet wide. About ten-feet from the right side of the cave was a sixty-foot drop off of the mountain. We were told that at the back of the cave, there was a hole carved out where you can see Al-Masjid Al-Haram, which was about five miles away. Pilgrims had gone in to look at the masjid and couldn't get out of the cave because of the crowd. No one was able to move in or out, just a bunch of pushing and shoving. We decided not to go near the cave and just watched from a distance. We definitely avoided the right side of the cave. After about a half hour, we decided to head back down and return to the house. It would have been nice to look through the hole in the back of the cave but not under those conditions. It was much too dangerous and we didn't want to risk getting hurt. I must say that it was a thrill to actually see the cave.

In the morning, we put on our ihrams and began our journey to the tent city of Mina. We had to stay in Mina the entire day until the Fajr prayer the next morning. As we walked to Mina, we met a mother and son from Maryland that we became good friends with. Some rode cars and buses but we traveled the traditional way, on foot. After talking with them, they revealed that they were Shi'ite Muslims and from our reactions, they explained why they thought that we should've been Shi'ites also. We explained why we shouldn't follow the Shi'ites and we left the subject alone. We both held a mutual respect for each other.

When we arrived in Mina, the first thing we had to do was to find a tent to rest our heads because the sun was devastating on our bodies. As far as we could look we saw white tents. The tents were sectioned off by countries. We found the USA section and chose our tent. The mom and son came along with us. We dropped our backpacks, prayed, and went out to meet more Muslims. We walked around and randomly asked Muslims where they were from. That resulted in many interesting conversations. The next morning after sunrise we proceeded to Mount Arafat where we would pray until sunset. This is where the Prophet Muhammad (Pbuh) gave his last sermon. Here we prayed for all of our friends and family by name. According to Islamic doctrine, anything that you pray for on Mount Arafat would be granted. I prayed that my wife and family would become Muslims, and asked if we could be blessed and successful in all of our endeavors.

When we arrived at Mount Arafat, it was time for the combined Dhuhr and Asr prayers. The sun was still unbearable and we prayed with a group that had a tent overhead. Once we started the prayer, we noticed something different about the way the group prayed. They were Shi'ite Muslims. We had been told in the past that if we prayed behind a Shi'ite kateeb, who lead the prayer, our prayers would not be accepted. After the prayer, we moved behind the tent and prayed again. The Shi'ite mother and son felt comfortable about the prayer. It was soon after the prayer that we found a place on Mount Arafat and began praying again. There were so many people there that it was hard to find a vacant spot. We climbed about thirty feet and found a small open spot. We sat there and started our supplications.

There was no shade on Arafat and this was the hottest part of the day. The Saudi government drove in trucks of Zam Zam water and fruits throughout the Hajj. They both came in handy to help keep us hydrated. On the way up and after we sat, we heard hundreds of voices praying and asking for forgiveness. Never had we seen so many people humble themselves as if they were standing in front of the Creator on the Day of Judgment. We remained on Arafat until sunset and then off we were to Muzdalifah where we would remain overnight until after the morning prayer.

When we left Arafat, we came to a four way intersection where the pilgrims were at a stand still. Pilgrims were pushing in all four directions trying to get through the intersection. The mother and son got caught in the pushing and shoving and started to get lost in the crowd. My brother and I held hands so that we would not separate. The mother and son drifted further and further away and we lost contact with them. We never saw them again during the Hajj.

Once in Muzdalifah, we prayed Maghrib and Isha prayers and began to look for a place to sleep. Muzdalifah was so crowded; it was hard to find a place to lie down. We searched over a quarter mile radius and couldn't find a place large enough for both of us to settle for the night. With fatigue setting in, we started to get desperate. We settled for a location that we didn't want to be, along side of a busy road. Knowing how dangerous this could be, we hardly slept at all. With cars, buses, and ambulances rolling by our heads, we tried to keep an eye on the oncoming traffic. We were right at the edge of the road, so morning could not come fast enough.

After the morning prayer, we were on our way to the city of Mina. While walking from Muzdalifah, we stopped to pick up seven small stones to throw at the stone pillar Al-Aqabah (the largest of the Jamarats). The Jamarats were located where Satan tried to tempt Abraham to stray from the straight path of Allah (swt). Abraham threw stones at Satan to ward him off. When we reached the Jamarat, we didn't begin to throw our stones until we could get close enough to the Jamarat without getting hit with stones from pilgrims who were behind us and couldn't reach the pillar. Although we were a good distance from the pillar, we still had to basically throw and duck to avoid getting hit. We repeated "Allahu Ahkbar," (God is great) upon throwing each stone. After the stoning of the Jamarat, we had to sacrifice a goat or lamb. We came to the location and you could see goats and lambs stretched out for a mile. You had the choice of slaughtering the animal yourself, or you could pay to have someone do it for you. We paid $75 to have it done for us. The meat from the animal was given to the poor and needy. The slaughtering of the goat is a re-enactment of Allah (swt) giving Abraham a ram to sacrifice instead of his son Ishmael that Abraham was willing to sacrifice because Allah (swt) had commanded him to do so. After the sacrifice, we had to shave our heads, make tawaf at the masjid again and remove our ihrams. After removing our ihrams, we headed back to Mina for the next two days to sleep under the stars.

The area of Mina where we were was just an open field with a few restroom facilities scattered throughout. With the volume of pilgrims there, the restroom lines were usually ten to fifteen minutes long. For the morning prayer, we had to make sure that we got up early enough so that we would have enough time to wash before the prayer. That afternoon, we had to stone the other three pillars where Abraham was tempted by Satan. In previous years, there had been stampedes there because of the volume of pilgrims so we had to be cautious while stoning the Jamarats. Thankfully, we managed to safely escape the Jamarats.

In keeping within the rules of Hajj, we had to leave Mina by sunset for our farewell tawaf around the Ka'bah. This was the last stage of the Hajj ritual. After tawaf we had to immediately leave the city of Mecca. We left Al-Masjid Al-Haram and headed back to the Indonesian's home where we had been staying. There our sponsor picked us up and transported us to Jeddah where we would catch our flight back to Malaysia. When our sponsor went to the Hajj office to pick up our passports, he was told that we couldn't get them until Hajj had officially ended. We were unaware of that when we booked our return flights. Apparently, we booked our return flights a day too early. The Saudi government was very strict about that and rarely did they compromise on their policy. We now faced the possibility of missing our flight back to Malaysia which was leaving in three hours. With the political pull that our sponsor had, he was able to convince the Hajj Ministry in about an hour to grant us the passports. We were then off to Jeddah to process out of Saudi Arabia and to catch our flight.

We stopped to enjoy some of the scenery in Jeddah. They had plush palaces everywhere and the waterfront areas were beautiful. After arriving at the airport, we processed out of Saudi Arabia with our passports and went to the gift shop to pick up some items that we didn't want to carry during the pilgrimage. We were told at the processing station that there were more than two million Hajj Pilgrims that year. Our sponsor presented us with gifts and then departed to see his family. We couldn't thank him enough for all that he had done to make the trip possible. He was working and living in Riyadh and his wife was working and living in Jeddah with the children. From Riyadh to Jeddah was a six-hour drive, and he was glad to drop us off in Jeddah. We patiently waited for our flight, reflecting back on our Hajj experience, looking forward to getting home to tell our stories to the families. That experience will definitely last a lifetime and it changed my life forever.

We arrived in Kuala Lumpur and we were picked up by the Embassy driver. We talked about our experience the entire forty-five minute drive. When we arrived at the house on the compound and met our friends we were staying with, we told the entire story again. After we ate and freshened up, we were back in the streets of Kuala Lumpur shopping. We were leaving the next day heading back to Okinawa so we had to complete our shopping lists. A couple of the items that we picked up, we mailed from the Embassy post office the next morning. On our previous trips to the Embassy, we had to endure long lines because of the locals who were trying to obtain visas, passports, and other U. S. Government documents. We remembered that my friend informed us that if we didn't have time to stand in the lines, just asked the guards for the "Gunny." Gunny was used for his Marine Corps rank of Gunnery Sergeant. Since he was the Detachment Commander there at the Embassy, he was in charge of the compound security. We walked to the front of the line and asked for the "Gunny." In less than a minute, the Gunny came out to the gate and took us inside. Our bags were packed and we were ready to complete the final leg of our Hajj journey back to Okinawa. We thanked our friends and said our goodbyes to his wonderful family for all of their hospitality and assistance to and from Saudi Arabia. It was a blessing that they were there and we thanked Allah (swt) for them. We were then off to the airport. The driver dropped us off, and we went directly to immigrations. The immigrations clerk recognized the Hajj stamps in our passports and began asking about the experience. As much as we tried to downplay the issue, they really made us feel like celebrities. We didn't want to hold up the lines so we talked as we walked through the processing station. They all seemed happy that we had made Hajj. We checked in our bags and waited for our flight.

We arrived in Okinawa and my brother's wife picked us up. She too received an ear full of our Hajj stories. A usual half hour trip from the airport seemed like it only took ten minutes because of the stories.

My wife and children barely recognized me when I walked into the house. Over the twenty-one days gone, I had grown a full mustache and goatee. This was the first time that they had ever seen hair on my face. I kept the mustache and goatee for that day but shaved it off the next morning before returning to work. My wife proudly showed me the books about Islam she read while I was gone. She said that she had learned more in those twenty-one days than she had the entire year. She shared the information with the children and they too had learned quite a bit. We stayed up pretty late talking about what they had learned and what I had gone through making Hajj. The next day after work I called the community brothers and informed them that we had returned. We all agreed to meet at the masjid to talk about the experience. I took some Zam Zam water that I had brought back in plastic containers for those who hadn't tasted it. We sat around in a circle and shared the Hajj experience with the brothers. The two brothers that had gone the year before could really relate to what we were feeling. I think that everyone there felt a good appreciation of Hajj, its meaning, and what it took to endure it and receive the spiritual fulfillment that it had to offer. A week later my prayers from Mount Arafat were answered by the grace of Allah (swt). My wife and youngest daughter took their shahadahs, or declarations of faith and became Muslims.

A week after returning to work, I called the Okinawa Marine (OKIMAR) Newspaper to see if they would be interested in writing a story about my experience. The Okinawa Marine was the authorized Department of Defense newspaper for Okinawa, Japan. They had published outstanding stories of Marines and Sailors on Okinawa since 1968. The writer I spoke with checked with his supervisor and he said that it would make a good story. We arranged a meeting at my office a few days later. He came to my office and we walked down to the conference room. He wasn't that familiar with the Hajj so I explained what it was and what it meant to the Muslims. I also explained the different stages and some of the terminology. After he had a good idea of what the Hajj was about, he started to ask more specific questions. We talked for about an hour and he said that he had enough for the story. He asked if he could take my photo praying and that was the picture he placed in the OKIMAR with a full page write-up that upcoming Friday when the paper was published. I saved a couple copies of the article and I sent a few home for the family.

"Hajj Pilgrims climbing Jabal Al Nur to see the cave where the Prophet Muhammad (Pbuh) used to go to meditate."

"The crowded cave entrance."

"Pilgrims at the Prophet's (Pbuh) Masjid in Madinah."

"The first structure of the Prophet's (Pbuh) Masjid in Madinah."

Sponsoring in Ethiopia

For years I had heard of the famine and diseases that plagued the people of Ethiopia. Although it was one of the poorest countries in the world, the people had hearts of gold. It's sad to say that most people couldn't show you where the country of Ethiopia was on a map, but they can tell you that the only thing they knew about Ethiopia was that the country produced some great distance runners that have made names for themselves in the long distance running circuit. I recall one Ethiopian runner who ran a 26.2 mile Olympic Marathon while barefoot. I can attest that another advantage of Islam was that it expanded knowledge of global events, cultures, and geography. I'd met so many Muslims from all corners of the world and it was interesting talking with them to get an idea of how it was growing up in their countries.

With our Muslim community doing so well there in Okinawa, we felt the need to do something to help the people of Ethiopia. We decided to sponsor a family through an organization called Islamic Relief that our community donated money to on a monthly basis, especially during Ramadan. Islamic Relief had sites set up in many of the poorest Muslim countries that unfortunately didn't have the resources to combat poverty, joblessness, poor water conditions, infant mortality, and a host of other issues that kept the country dependent on outside sources. We researched the organization and then their Orphan Sponsorship Program for details. Through Islamic Relief, we could sponsor an orphan family from about 15 or 20 countries, and the monthly amount paid depended on the country where the family resided. The Prophet Muhammad (Pbuh) conveyed throughout the Quran that we must take care of the orphans. He, himself was once an orphan that was taken in by his uncle. For a very reasonable amount of money, a family in Ethiopia could be provided food, water, education, and at times clothing. In turn, Islamic Relief would send our community photos and information of the family and their progress. All correspondence was routed through Islamic Relief for legal reasons. We decided to sponsor an Ethiopian family and we notified Islamic Relief of our intentions. When the organization responded, they sent a detailed package of the sponsorship program and many of the other programs that they administered around the world.

About two weeks later, we received photos and information about the family that desperately needed our help. It was a widow with four children whose husband had passed due to medical complications. The photos and information on the family were shared with the community after Jummah (Friday prayers). Every month or so, Islamic Relief would send us an update on how the family was doing. The community sponsored the family until July of 2002 when my family transferred back to the states.

Moroccan Hospitality

During my eleven years spent in Okinawa, Japan, I've had the pleasure of serving with six brothers from Morocco, five of which I'm still in contact with today. Three of these brothers were Marines and three were Navy. Five of these brothers have left a lasting impression on my heart that has had a critical impact on how I feel about Moroccan culture. While they each often told us stories about Fez, Marrakesh, Meknes, and Casablanca, they all touched my heart in a special way. One is now employed as an Executive Accountant on Wall Street in New York City. He served as a Navy Corpsman, who were our lifeline on the battlefield. When I asked him why he was getting out of the Navy, he told me that he wanted to pursue a degree in accounting and he did just that.

Another brother took time out of his weekends to teach the community Arabic. The brother spoke four languages and he was learning Japanese at the time. He also prepared Moroccan food for us whenever we had social gatherings. Brother three was a heavy vehicle operator in the Corps. He enlisted in the Corps without knowing one full sentence of English. He was given the opportunity to come to the United States by way of Denver, Colorado from a lottery in Morocco. A specified number of Moroccans were given lottery cards by the government.

He arrived in Denver and only knew one person there who tried to teach him English in just one week prior to enlisting in the military. He guessed the answers on the Armed Forces Vocational Aptitude Battery (ASVAB) Test and scored high enough to enter the service. He was able to make it through boot camp by listening and repeating what he heard his platoon members saying. The will and the drive he had to succeed was amazing. He also taught us Arabic and after four years in the Corps, he decided to leave the Corps in order to obtain his Bachelor's degree. He returned to Okinawa three years later, after he married a young lady who landed a job at the Japanese University teaching Spanish. I was fortunate enough to witness this brother walk across the stage receiving his bachelor's degree from the University of Maryland.

The fourth brother, a Marine at one of the neighboring bases, worked for one of my friends at the unit's warehouse. He was an impeccable example of a Marine. His work ethic, moral standards and good character stood out amongst all of the Marines in his section. After he transferred back to the states, he was replaced by another Muslim. Whenever the new brother asked for time off to attend Friday prayers or special favors, my friend would not hesitate to grant it. He often said to the new Marine, "If you're anything like the Marine you replaced, just let me know what you need." The Moroccan brother set that type of an example. He was also a blessing to the Muslim community because he helped to recite the Quran for our Holy Month of Ramadan, where we would complete one part of the Quran per night for thirty nights.

The fifth brother has made such an impact on my life as well as my family we felt that we were Honorary Moroccans. He worked as a Navy dental technician while stationed in Okinawa. He too helped to recite the Quran for us during Ramadan. He once told me that if my family and I ever had the desire to go to Morocco, to let him know and he would make arrangements with his family in Morocco to accommodate us. We often heard people say this, but did they really mean it?

About eight months after he transferred from Okinawa, my family and I made plans to go home to Virginia for thirty days. We also decided that while we were home, we would take the brother's offer and travel to Morocco. Through our acquaintances, we had heard so much about Morocco that we had to experience it for ourselves. I lived thirty minutes from the Naval Base in Norfolk, Virginia that had free military flights weekly to the base in Rota, Spain. We could rent a car there and drive down to the most southern city of Spain, Algeciras, and then catch the ferry through the Strait of Gibraltar to Morocco. That was our game-plan, but the hard part was telling our families that we would only be home for four days before flying out to Spain. We hadn't seen our families for a year, but a trip to Morocco would outweigh the hurt feelings of the loved ones. They later understood how much the trip meant to us. My mother had traveled the world while my father was in the military, but my wife's family had never been out of the United States.

After arriving home for vacation, we quickly made our rounds to see everyone. That was accomplished in two days and while we were in Norfolk visiting, we stopped by the Naval Base to submit our paperwork for the next flight out to Spain. The Air Mobility Command (AMC) Terminal had two flights leaving in two days. We returned in two days with our luggage excited about our trip. Once inside the terminal we noticed that there were two flights leaving for Spain that morning. We had to wait for the space available call which was approaching in an hour. Flights or missions-as the terminal personnel call them-are loaded with cargo first and if they have space available after the cargo, they open up seats for passengers. These flights were free of charge and they could transport you to many bases in the continental United States and countries abroad. It was a great way to travel if you had a lot of time on your hands. If there weren't any space available flights headed to your destination, there was always low cost lodging on the bases for your families. Patience was always a plus when it came to traveling in space available status. When it was time for space available call, the terminal personnel announced that they had quite a few seats available for Rota, Spain. We had six family members traveling so we were pretty confident that we would make the flight.

We left our six-month old granddaughter with my mother, as it was an inconvenience to travel with her for that distance. We were manifested for the flight but the flight would stop at Dover, Air Force Base, Delaware for a day, and then continue to Rota, Spain the following day. This gave us the opportunity to spend a day in Dover, a place we hadn't been before. It was only an hour flight to Dover and as soon as we claimed our luggage, we were off to billeting for rooms. The flight crew and staff gave us the time to show up the following day. We didn't venture too far from billeting. The Exchange, Commissary, and gymnasium were all located in the same vicinity. We returned to the terminal the next day for our flight to Rota. It was a seven hour flight to Rota and we were pretty excited to get there. We rented two cars at the terminal. All of their cars were compacts and there was no way that six of us could get into one car.

The Navy Lodge was where we could rest our heads for this stage of the trip. We checked in and then went off the base for some sight-seeing. The city of Rota was really beautiful, enriched with Spanish heritage and culture. Their heritage and culture were reflected on the base as well. We sat down that evening to map out our plan for Morocco. We spotted a few travel agencies while we were out and noted their locations. The next day, we were there inquiring about the best way to travel to Morocco. Since we had rental cars, they instructed us to drive to the most southern city in Spain, Algeciras, and catch the ferry. We paid the agency for our ferry tickets and grabbed a map of Morocco for directions to Casablanca. Next, we exchanged American dollars for Moroccan currency, or dirhams.

We headed south on a one and a half hour trip down to southern Spain. Traveling through the countryside was spectacular. We passed through countless farms with plentiful herds of healthy cattle and horses. We rode up and down the mountains trying to guess what our altitude was. We also noticed why Spain is famous for its wine. Vineyards stretched across much of the Spanish soil from the time we departed Rota, until almost into Algeciras. When we arrived at the ferry dock, the lines of cars had already started forming. We had about an hour before the next one arrived. There was nothing to do on the dock so we just waited in the car.

When the ferry arrived, we had to wait until the vehicles disembarked. It was a very large ferry and we could see why it took so long. Once on board, we took a look around to see what the ferry had to offer. There were about three or four decks we could explore. We realized that one deck had food and another was utilized for processing into the country, which is where we had to get our passports stamped. While going through the process, the gentleman noticed that I had a Hajj stamp inside my passport, meaning that I had made the pilgrimage to Mecca, Saudi Arabia. He immediately told the others and they began to ask me how it was. Their whole demeanor changed and it seemed like they rolled out the red carpet for us. Once we left that deck, it was back to normal.

On the upper deck, we were told that we would travel through the Strait of Gibraltar and that this would allow us the opportunity to see the Rock of Gibraltar. I'd heard about the rock but I knew nothing about its significance, or if it had any significance at all. While venturing around each deck, we heard Spanish, French, and Arabic conversations. My interest was to try to guess where everyone was from. I could guess the Moroccan females because most of them wore the long jallaba which is a long dress with a hood. I could pretty much guess the French females because they wore less conservative clothing. It was very hard to guess the males, except for their complexion of either white for European French or a mixture of African and European for the Moroccans.

Soon we received the announcement that we were docking in the city of Tangier in Morocco. The first thing that I had to do after we disembarked was to call my brother's family to let them know that we were in Tangier. It dawned on me then that this was our first time on African soil. We had finally touched our Motherland. We had arrived just before sunset and then darkness had started to set in.

The streets were very crowded in Tangier. This was the time of the day when everyone came out to shop, eat and to enjoy the night life. Vendors were walking up to the cars as we stopped for traffic. We stopped at one location to grab some souvenirs and then we were back on the road. We drove a couple of hours until we got tired and we stopped at a roadside motel to sleep. Prior to reaching the motel, we stopped at a roadside store to get something to eat. The storekeeper could not speak English and I spoke neither French nor Arabic. I tried talking with some Moroccan men and boys who were at the back of the store but they didn't speak English either. They did understand when I told them that we were Muslims. Then the few Arabic words that I knew came in handy. They were very receptive and appreciated the fact that we had come to their country. I got a warm feeling from the bunch and I thought to myself that if that's the way the people are here in Morocco, then we're going to have a wonderful trip. I paid for our products in a language that we both could understand, dirhams (Moroccan currency). We greeted each other and then we departed.

The next morning we were up early and on the road. My son had the roadmap so he was navigating while I drove. My wife drove the other vehicle. As we traveled along the highway, we saw a big difference between the scenery of Morocco and the scenery we had seen in Spain. In Spain we saw large horse and cattle farms with healthy livestock, but in Morocco it was the complete opposite. Here we saw a patch of cows sporadically and a few horses. We even passed a few camels trotting through the sand on the beach. The livestock didn't look healthy at all in Morocco. Off from a distance we saw what looked to be a castle or fortress of some sort. It was located in the city of Assilah. We stopped there to take a look. Inside the fortress were many shops of vendors selling everything from carpets, to clothing, fruits and vegetables, gold and silver. We looked at the Moroccan carpets but we couldn't tell if we were getting a good price or not, so we moved on. Although there were many things to purchase there, we decided to wait until we got to Casablanca before we would do any shopping.

We soon left Assilah for the capital city Rabat. After arriving in Rabat, we drove around to look at some of the sights and then we were back on the road. I really wanted to go to the American Embassy in Rabat but we were anxious to get to Casablanca. When we arrived in Casablanca, we looked for a hotel to settle in prior to calling my brother's family. I called his sister from the lobby and she said that she would be there in about twenty minutes. I called another brother's family also because he too told me to call his family once we arrived in Casablanca.

My brother's sister arrived first and we recognized her immediately because they looked so much alike. My other brother's cousin arrived about ten minutes after she did. We were then involved in a tug of war. They both wanted us to come to their houses. They were speaking Arabic but I could tell that it was not a good conversation. These were people that had never seen us in their lives. I intervened in the conversation and told them that we would go to both of their houses. Then the conversation shifted to which one we would go to first. They decided that we would visit the cousin's home first and then my brother's family's home.

When we walked into their home, we could smell the aroma of Moroccan food. We met his wife and son before entering a large living area decorated in traditional Moroccan colors and furniture. There was a large sheet spread out on the floor with an assortment of foods, breads, and desserts. I said to myself that there was no way that we could eat that much food but we definitely gave it a try. After we ate, we were treated with Moroccan tea as we sat and chatted with the family.

In a couple of hours we decided to visit the other family. My brother's cousin took us to their home. When we arrived there, it was the same scenario. We met his four brothers, his cousin, his mother, and of course his sister again. We walked into their sitting area and they too had a large spread of food waiting for us. We explained that we had eaten at the other house but they insisted that we eat there. We couldn't eat as much there as we did at the other house but we still managed to put most of it away. When we finished dinner, we were able to relax with Moroccan tea again. By that time, the long day was starting to take a toll on us so I told the family that it was time to go to the hotel. They insisted that we stay at their home. Again, these were people who had never met us before, and they were opening up their home to us. They told us where each of us would sleep and it didn't take long after that for us to call it a night.

We were up early the next morning for a full day of excitement. Their mother and sister made breakfast and then we were off for a day of sight-seeing and shopping. They took us to a large market place where there were endless shops and vendors. We shopped for tea sets and clothing. Once we completed our shopping, they took us to the third largest masjid in the Muslim world, Masjid Hassan II. It was designed by a French architect and it sat next to the Atlantic Ocean, which could be seen through a gigantic glass floor. There was also a huge library that was connected to the masjid, and a stone walk-way that could accommodate 80,000 people. As I always did, I had to go inside to pray in it. I tried to pray at least one time in every masjid I saw. I prayed two rakahs and we left for another market and then to the house.

We sat at the house that night and talked with the family. We talked about famous places and people in the United States. They asked questions about living in the U.S. and we asked about living in Morocco. They expressed their desire to someday go to college in the states as their older brother did, who was still in the Navy at that time. We told them that we would love to purchase a home there in Morocco and be able to visit any time while vacationing. Their prices for real estate were very reasonable in American currency.

They had a very close family. We saw photos of their father who had passed away, but we didn't ask any questions about him because we didn't know how sensitive it would be. They showed a great deal of respect for their mother and it seemed like every time they had the chance, they would either hug her or kiss her. I have never witnessed an American family act this way with that much respect, love and affection for one's mother.

We spent our next day in Morocco preparing for our return trip to the United States. First, we had to get back to Rota, and wait for a flight heading back to Norfolk, Virginia. We were up early the following morning to say our goodbyes and to thank the wonderful family for making our first trip to the African continent a successful one and an experience that we would remember forever. That had to be the best trip that my family and I had taken yet. I told them that I would call their brother when we returned to the states and let him know that Moroccan hospitality was second to none.

We set off only saddened that we couldn't stay longer but the thought registered that we had only spent three days with our families after being gone for a year in Japan. We gassed up the previous night so we were ready to head north to Tangier. We only stopped a couple of times on our way to Tangier to stretch. It seemed like it took us less time to get back. When we arrived, the ferry was not there so we waited down at the dock just as we did on our way down. Soon we were on board and heading back through the Strait to Algeciras.

On the ferry we had our passports stamped again certifying that we had departed Morocco. While on the ferry, we toured the different levels and then relaxed for the hour and a half ride back to Rota. Soon we were docking again waiting in line to disembark. When we touched Spanish soil, we found the dock gate and then the highway leading back to Cadiz and then Rota. My three daughters slept while my son stayed awake to navigate.

By the time we reached Rota, we were exhausted from the trip and the excitement of going back home. We stopped by the terminal to see when the next flight was departing for Norfolk. There were no planes scheduled to leave that day so we checked back into the Navy Lodge and turned in our rental cars. We spent the rest of the day catching up on our rest so that we could get up early and go back to the terminal to check on flights. There were a couple of flights scheduled later the next day and it seemed like they had available seats to accommodate the people waiting in the terminal. We managed to catch the first flight out because most of the people who arrived before us were heading to Italy and Germany. We were glad to be on our way back home. It was an exhausting trip. Although the MD-11 plane was cold going back, I still slept so peacefully.

When I did wake up, I reflected back on the trip thinking about how much of an experience it was. We had been to Spain and the North African country of Morocco. How many ordinary families can say that they've done that? How many families coming from small cities like ours would even fathom doing it? We came away from this trip realizing that trips like that were very educational for our families. We developed a deep respect and appreciation for the Moroccan culture that we had heard so much about; a culture deep in multi-ethnic diversity disseminating from the Berbers, Jewish, Arabs, and Moors, with top priorities to protect its diversity and preservation of its cultural heritage. We definitely looked forward to taking more trips to other countries sometime in the near future.

"Walida prepared lunch Moroccan style during her visit to San Diego in 2009."

"Part of our Moroccan Family from Casablanca, now residing in San Diego."

Bosnian and Herzegovina Freedom Fighters

Upon arriving to our prayer room (musallah) at the Camp Foster Chapel, I noticed an unfamiliar face on the walk-way approaching the room. I introduced myself and he did likewise, saying that his unit 1st Battalion, 3rd Marines, an infantry battalion from Hawaii, had just arrived on Okinawa on their six-month Unit Deployment Program (UDP). He was informed by his chain of command that Islamic services were held there on Camp Foster. The brother was from Bosnia and Herzegovina. This was the second brother that I had met from that region. I met the other a couple years back at that same location.

About a month after being on the island, the Okinawa Marine, the base newspaper, featured an article on the brother that opened my eyes to the atrocities that the Bosnians faced during the Bosnian War of 1992-95.

The full page article revealed his picture and explained that that region of Yugoslavia was divided by three ethnic groups, the Catholic Croats, the Orthodox Christian Serbs, and the Bosnian Muslims. The Bosnian Muslims declared independence from Yugoslavia but the Bosnian Serbs rejected the declaration. After the independence was granted, the Bosnian Serbs, backed by the Federal Republic of Yugoslavia, sought out to rid Eastern Bosnia of the non-Serb population, primarily the Muslims. The Serbs went on a campaign of ransacking and burning houses and apartments belonging to Muslims. The Croats and Muslims made an alliance but most Croats were driven from the cities with Muslim majorities. Men, women, and children were placed in camps and many were killed. A large majority of the Muslim women were raped and physically abused. Bosnian Muslims were easy targets because they were poorly equipped and not prepared for war.

During the last part of the war, there were reports of eyewitness accounts of Bosnian men, women, and children being taken to large pits, being shot and killed, and bull-dozed into the pits for burial in the city of Srebrenica. These accounts shocked the world. The acts of genocide got the attention of the United Nations and subsequently resulted in air strikes against Serb and Yugoslav forces. Shortly afterward, the presidents of Bosnia, Serbia, and Croatia signed the Dayton Agreement to halt all fighting between the three ethnic groups. The Bosnian government charged Serbia with genocide but the Serbs were exonerated. The judges ruled that the criteria for genocide with specific intent to destroy Bosnian Muslims were met only in Srebrenica or Eastern Bosnia in 1995. They did, however, rule crimes against humanity. The Bosnian government reported that 8,000 boys and men between the ages of 13 to 77 were killed during the conflict. Many non-combatant Muslims also died from hunger and exposure to the elements.

Many people across the globe had no idea that this conflict even existed. Most could never imagine how life was growing up in a war-torn society. Sacrificing your childhood to defend your way of life does not describe the life of most men over the course of their lifetime. This brother, along with his younger brother who was also a Marine had to defend their culture, ethnicity, and religion as teenagers in the Bosnia War. This was the very reason why they both joined the Marine Corps.

Their country is now divided into three ethnic divisions with heavily armed United Nations forces patrolling to maintain order. Life was more stable in Bosnia but tensions still had the potential to escalate into conflict again. Memory of the past still haunted many of its citizens, especially those who lost family members. During the conflict, U.S. Immigrations sent many Bosnians to the United States as refugees to escape atrocities.

Here in the U.S. their lives were started from nothing, living in foster homes and shelters until the Bosnians were able to find employment and sustain their families.

The brother is now a Staff Sergeant serving as a Non-Lethal Weapons Instructor and Training Chief for Marine Forces Europe in Germany. I was unable to locate his younger brother whom I served with in Okinawa as well, until he transferred to Kansas City, Missouri in 2007.

For many countries, freedom does not come easy. What we take for granted in America, other countries can't guarantee on a day-to-day basis. Both brothers were given a new outlook on life and the opportunity for them and their families to enjoy the freedoms that I speak of. Although the memories of their war-struck teenage lives may linger, they can now look back and say that they did what they had to do for their country. I am proud to have served with both of them.

The Muslim Chinese Army Chaplain

In March of 2000, my niece and her family were stationed at the Ft. Lewis Army Base in Tacoma, Washington. I had talked with her a few weeks back about my interest in going out there to visit. There were flights out of Kadena to Seattle International Airport and it wouldn't cost anything. I talked with her again to arrange a visit in a couple of weeks.

I arrived for a week's stay but I ran out of things to do. The weather was cold and rainy so that eliminated outside activities. Friday was approaching so I decided that I would attend Friday prayers if Islamic services were offered at the base. I utilized her computer to access the base website. Surprisingly, they offered Islamic services and there was a phone number listed for the Chaplain's office. I called to confirm the time and location. My niece offered to drop me off and to pick me up after service.

The services were held at the Base Chapel. I walked in and there were quite a few Muslims present, male and female. The Chaplain looked to be Malaysian or Indonesian. The majority of the Muslims were military but I could tell that there were a few civilians in attendance also. After service we gathered in a large room to socialize and get acquainted. I made my way to the Chaplain to see where he was from. He was of Chinese descent and his parents migrated to New Jersey probably because of the political unrest in China at that time, but he didn't say. They opened a dry cleaning business which was able to support the family. The Chaplain was a West Point Army Academy graduate. I do remember him saying that he went to Syria to learn Arabic and Islamic Studies. He was a very humble brother with extensive knowledge about Islam and had an incredible drive for enjoining the good and forbidding the evil. This was one of the traits that Muslims strive for. He told me about some of his experiences while in pursuit to become a Chaplain and I must say that it was a challenge that most would have succumbed to. His life was a very interesting story.

As I moved across the room to meet others, I noticed a brother who looked African. I walked over to see where he was from. Nigeria was his country but he entered into the U. S. and joined the Army. He had an interesting story to tell as well, from growing up in Nigeria. While talking to one of the African American brothers, I noticed that he had the same last name as one of the brothers I served with in 1997 in Okinawa. I asked if they were related and he said that the Muslim I served with was his son. What a coincidence! I recall him telling me back then that his father and brother were living in Seattle. His brother didn't attend service that day but it was a pleasure to meet his father. The father attended a local masjid there in Tacoma and occasionally came to the base. The Muslims there were very active in the local community, particularly with food and clothing programs. It was always good to hear that the Muslims are taking an active part in building a stronger society.

When I returned to my niece's house, I called the brother to let him know that I had met his father. He transferred from Okinawa in 1999 and was then stationed in Florida.

A Look at Military Life

As the military brothers became more acquainted with the students at the Okinawa International Center (OIC), we started to think of ways that could make their stay on Okinawa more enjoyable. Many of the students attending the OIC were married and had children that they left back in their countries. They were provided internet access at the OIC and they purchased phone cards from stores in the vicinity. This was how they communicated to their families back home. Accommodations at the facility also included a gymnasium with badminton, volleyball, basketball, a swimming pool, a game room with table tennis and pool tables, a karaoke room, a lounge with a television on every floor, and a soccer field.

The students were not permitted to drive so they had to rely on public transportation or taxi cabs to gain access to the wide variety of sights on Okinawa. The OIC scheduled field trips to various attractions on the island which helped the students to learn the language and culture of the host country. The students from each course were given a project to have completed their final week at the OIC but that wasn't very time consuming for most of them considering that they already had degrees in their fields which made things much easier.

With all of this in mind and after answering questions about how we lived on the bases, we decided to bring a group of students on the base to show them how we lived. Most of the students didn't know much about the American military but they gave us a great deal of respect, probably from what they had heard or seen on television. Some looked at the U. S. as a bully nation because they thought that we were always trying to enforce our policies on countries whose forces were not able to effectively defend themselves. This was a good opportunity for us to show the students from the other countries that in most cases America had good intentions. Our conversations with the Arabs and Iranians, really opened our eyes to U. S. activities that were taking place on their soil that we probably would never have heard about.

My plan was to have one of the military brothers ride with me and we would pick up as many students as we could get in my van. I could usually fit about seven average size people in it. First we would give them a tour of the base, then we would take them to the Base Exchange for some shopping, and lastly we would take them to the food court for dinner.

The next Saturday, I called one of the OIC brothers to let him know that we were coming to pick them up. When we arrived, there was a group of about ten students waiting to go. I apologized and told them that I could only get about seven into the van per base regulations. They picked those who could make the trip and I promised the others that we would do the same the following weekend. All of the students who made the trip that day were not Muslims. Although they had only been at the OIC for about two weeks, the Christians had already learned a great deal about the Islamic faith. For many of the Christians at the OIC, this was their first experience interacting with Muslims. They had a great deal of respect for the faith but they felt that we had too many rules, (i.e. no drinking, no eating pork, no boyfriends/girlfriends, no skimpy clothes, and that praying five times a day was too much). They said that once before you go to bed at night was enough. We often explained to them that eating pork was forbidden in the Bible as well and they didn't even know it. I found myself taking my Bible to the OIC to show them some of the inconsistencies. As for the women dressing provocatively, we asked them how did the mother of Jesus (Pbuh) dress? Most understood but there were some who told us that we weren't back in those times.

Since most of them were Catholic, we mentioned that the Nuns dressed like the mother of Jesus (Pbuh), and they began to accept the fact then. For praying five times a day, we asked them to compare that to taking five baths a day. After five baths a day, you're going to be pretty clean, same concept with praying. Although all the singles had boyfriends/girlfriends, they understood why it was forbidden in Islam. With the size of the OIC and the day to day interaction with the Muslims, most of the non-Muslims left the OIC with an extensive knowledge about Islam. There were some that wanted to become Muslim before going back to their countries but they didn't know how their families would react. The others didn't care.

There were two bases that we primarily took them to. One was the Camp Foster Marine Base and the other was the larger Kadena Air Force Base. Kadena had a larger Base Exchange but Camp Foster had a better food court. If we went to Camp Foster I would also take them through Futenma Air Station, so that they could see the aircrafts, especially the Cobra Attack Helicopters. The Air Station was located a half mile from Camp Foster. We hardly ever saw the helicopters operating.

When we arrived at the base we showed them most of the facilities that attracted folks to the base, like the commissary, the theater, swimming pool, gymnasium, and the club where we exchanged dollars for Japanese currency. We always managed to show them our musallah or small masjid where we regularly congregated for prayers. Next we went to the Base Exchange for some shopping. The only requirement for their entry into the Exchange was to sign them in the guest book at the door. Then, the brother took one group and I took the other. That way we could answer their questions easier. The ladies would always go to the perfumes and fragrances and the men would go to the electronics. The men who were married would visit the perfumes also on the way out. Their most popular items were video cameras, nintendos, and laptop computers. Although they could purchase those items at selected Japanese stores, they chose to buy them on the base. The prices were somewhat similar. Once both groups had a basket of products, we were off to the register. Exchange policy is that you must show a military identification card to purchase, so I gathered the money from my group and my brother did the same for his. Everything always worked out fine.

The third stage of our tour was always to visit our food court for dinner. We tried to focus on one item that everyone would like, pizza. Although they served pizza at the OIC, it was not that good and everyone missed the pizza from their homelands. We ordered six large cheese pizzas. The Muslims don't eat pork so we didn't bother with sausage and pepperonis. We're not even allowed to eat the pizza if it has one pepperoni, one piece of ham or one piece of sausage on it. The grease from those meats was considered pork also. The Muslims would even ask if we could ask the cooks to wash the pizza cutters before cutting our pizza, because they used the same cutters to slice pork on previous pizzas. The cooks always obliged. Most of the students had never tasted root beer soda and when I mentioned the word "root beer," the Muslim students told me that I knew that they couldn't drink alcohol. I then explained what root beer was. They loved the drink and the explanation.

For the occasions when no one had the desire for pizza, we took the students to the Istanbul Kabaab House owned by a Turkish Brother that lived in Chatan, very near to the base. He relocated the restaurant from the hustle and bustle of Naha City, to a location much nearer to the military clientele, where he entertained a constant flow of new faces transferring to and visiting Okinawa. At one time he operated two locations in Chatan.

The Istanbul Kabaab House offered a wide range of Turkish dishes and desserts, along with tea and coffee. He had an authentic Turkish cook that didn't speak English but always had a smile on his face when he saw us. Many days I called to let the owner know that I was stopping by for soup and tea. He never charged me for them.

I even took my office there for going-away parties. That way, most of them had their first opportunity to learn a little Turkish culture. The owner played videos about Turkey for entertainment and he had a collection of books about Turkey on display for purchase.

It was then time to return the students to the OIC. We loaded into the van with the back full of products. They talked about their experience the entire trip back. They really enjoyed themselves and couldn't wait to get back to tell the others. We were happy that we had the opportunity to show them how we lived in the military. I was already reassured that the next weekend would lead too much of the same thing.

"The Owner and Head Chef at the Turkish Istanbul Kabaab House in Okinawa, Japan."

Eid Ul Fitr 2000

Eid Ul Fitr is the Islamic celebration after the Muslim's month of fasting called Ramadan. In the year 2000 in Okinawa, Japan, the three Islamic communities coordinated probably the best Eid Feast that ever took place on Okinawa. In the previous years, we utilized a location on the Ryukyu University campus but it wasn't sufficient space to accommodate the three communities and their guests. The Military Community wanted to do something special that year. We discussed the possibility of having the celebration on the base in our Chapel Multi-Purpose Building, which was large enough to accommodate everyone. In addition to the space, it had a large kitchen, multiple rest rooms, and a play room for the children. We communicated our intentions to the brothers of the other two communities so they could get some feedback from those who would be involved with the logistics and planning.

We decided to do a potluck, that way the burden of cooking wouldn't be on just one community. Both off-base communities thought that it would be a good idea. Now that it was a plan, the military community had a number of tasks to complete in order to make this event happen. We had to submit a request to utilize the Multi-Purpose Building that day. All of the faith groups had access to the building for special events. We also had to request permission from Base Security to bring our guests on to the base. We anticipated resistance there because we were bringing Muslims from other countries on the base. We requested permission from the Camp Kinser Dining Facility to utilize their dishes, silver-ware, utensils, table covers and napkins, food warmers and candles. One of the military brothers was good friends with the dining facility manager and he offered the use of the items if needed. That made it easy for us to get access to the items we needed. The biggest logistical challenge we had was transporting students from the OIC and the university. Although some of the students at the university had transportation, the OIC students were not permitted to drive during their stay in Okinawa. That meant that the three of us that had vans would have to shuttle students from both locations which were roughly eight miles from the base.

Everything was approved but Base Security requested that we provide them with a list of everyone who was coming aboard the base and the license plate numbers for the cars that were being driven. We contacted our counterparts at the OIC and university and asked them to compile lists of everyone that would be attending. Once we received the lists, we provided the gate a copy and told them that we would have someone at the gate to sign everyone in on the date of the event.

We had a Muslim Chaplain at that time and he suggested that we invite the Commanding General and the Base Chaplain to the feast. This would be the first time that members of another faith group were invited to the Eid celebration. The Muslim Chaplain was responsible for sending out the invitations and surprisingly the Commanding General accepted. The Base Chaplain for the base also said that he would attend. This meant that now we had to follow proper protocol, which meant that the Muslim Chaplain was responsible for making sure that the General felt comfortable during his visit. He would greet him at his arrival and would escort him until his departure.

As the days came closer to the feast, we made final preparations for the event. We had sisters who volunteered to watch the children in the play room, brothers who volunteered to shuttle people to and from their locations, brothers to stay for cleanup, and brothers to direct those who were driving to the Multi-Purpose Building. I volunteered to be the Master of Ceremony since I knew most of the brothers and sisters from the other two communities.

On the morning of the feast we started early at the Multi-Purpose Building. We cleaned it and arranged the tables while the brother was on his way from the Dining Facility with the items he was promised we could borrow. We arranged every table the same, including the head table where the Commanding General would sit. We had everything completed in a matter of three hours. Next, we all departed to get dressed and we would launch the first vehicles to the OIC and university upon our return. Before they returned we had two brothers go to the gate to sign everyone in. The remainder of the military community stayed at the Multi-Purpose Building to entertain our guests as they arrived. Our Chaplain waited outside for the General. Everything worked out fine with no glitches.

Once everyone arrived and was seated, I took the microphone and thanked everyone for attending. I had to follow protocol and recognize the General and the Base Chaplain for attending also. Next, I wanted to go over the sequence of events before everyone commenced eating. The food was being placed on the burners as it was brought in and the aroma had already started to fill the air. There was a wide assortment of foods to choose from because of the different ethnic groups that were in attendance. We started serving as we did with all of our Islamic events with the women and children served first.

Once everyone was finished with their meals, I took my place at the microphone again for a few announcements. I wanted to make sure that our guests knew that we had just finished the month of Ramadan and that fasting was done to give us the same feeling of those who did not have food to eat. I also wanted to convey that because the Quran was revealed during the month of Ramadan, over two-thirds of the Muslims present had read the entire Quran during the thirty days of Ramadan. Next was to explain the concept of why we paid zakat, where 2.5 percent of our annual savings was donated to charitable organizations and needy families all over the world.

At our gathering, we had Muslim representation from twenty-one countries, ranging from the Middle East, the Far East and Africa. It was wonderful to see so many diverse cultures at the same gathering, each wearing their traditional clothing. Some of these countries were the poorest in the world. These were the places where the zakat money was most beneficial. Because prayer time was approaching, I wanted to conclude the feast to give our guests the opportunity to mingle and leave before the adhan was called. The Chaplain then took the General around to meet some of the Muslims and find out what countries they were from. Once the General made his rounds and then departed, the call to prayer was sounded. The prayer concluded the last portion of the feast. Now it was time to return the students to the OIC and university, then clean the Multi-Purpose Building.

It took about two hours to shuttle everyone back to their domiciles. Now we faced the biggest task. We folded tables and stacked chains in order to clean the floor for sweeping and mopping. About eight of us started washing the items that were loaned from the Dining Facility and once clean, we loaded everything in the van to be transported back there. We all worked like a well oiled machine until our mission was accomplished.

The entire evolution went just as planned with no flaws. We took on an immense logistical challenge and came out successful. We were confident that everyone enjoyed themselves and we felt that our guests left with a greater respect of Islam and the people who represented it. Who could we have shared this with better than the Commanding General who was a devout Christian? We left that evening with confidence that he would share this experience with his leadership at all levels.

Women in Islam

The Jewish, Christian, Hindu, and Muslim communities maintained a good relationship while utilizing the Camp Foster Base Chapel. We had several inter-faith lunches and dinners and we shared in community projects as well like orphanages and senior citizen's homes. The purpose of the inter-faith gatherings was to share the different aspects of each faith and to help bridge the gap between the respective faith groups.

As I walked to our musallah one day, I was approached by the Chapel Pastor and a couple of sisters from the Gospel community. The Pastor, who was female, asked if I could do a lecture for their congregation on Women in Islam. An incident that lead to this took place at an inter-faith dinner where they noticed that the Muslim women did not shake hands with any males, including the Muslim males. In Islam, this could be considered as a form of flirtation. Many of them had heard different things about Muslim women and they wanted to satisfy their curiosity. I told them that I would be glad to and we agreed on a date that was convenient for her congregation.

On the day of the lecture, there were about thirty ladies present. I started my lecture by thanking the Christian congregation for giving me the opportunity to speak on behalf of my Muslim sisters. My objective was to convey to them that much of what they had heard about Muslim women were misconceptions. I also informed them that it was always more beneficial to go to the source and I asked the question, "If you had eye problems, would you visit an optometrist or cardiologist?" Of course you would see the optometrist. That was to convey to them that if they had questions about women in Islam then they should confide in the Muslims for answers. I found that many non-Muslim sources were very misleading, whether intentionally or unintentionally. I went on to warn them that much of the reference material available at that time written by non-Muslims was responsible for many of the misconceptions about Muslim women and Islam in general. I directed them to some good websites that would give them accurate information on every aspect of the religion.

One of the biggest misconceptions about Muslim women is that they are not liberated and are oppressed because of the way that they're required to dress. Muslim women dress in this manner because they are taught the Islamic principle of guarding their modesty. You don't see that exercised too much in our society. Most of the Christian women felt that the Muslim women were oppressed until I asked why they didn't feel the same way about nuns. You couldn't hear one sound out of the Christians. Nuns have dressed like that for centuries.

What I had gathered from talking to Christians about Islam is that it is more effective to show them the verses in the Bible that verify what we try to teach them. I referred to the verse where it stated that women should cover their hair and they acknowledged the verse. One sister from the Christian congregation stated that she pays too much money to get her hair done so she was not going to cover it up. Another stated that she was going to adhere to what the Bible said and start covering hers. Not surprisingly, I saw her a couple weeks later and her hair was not covered. Perhaps she was persuaded to do otherwise.

Through some of the examples I gave and verses from the Quran and Bible, I was able to show them that Muslim women are held in high esteem in Islam and that they were considered the pillars of our communities. They had a young lady in their congregation from Sierra Leone, West Africa who was a Muslim prior to coming to the states. She confirmed what I conveyed to them. She also stated to me that I had done my homework on the subject matter. Listen to what the Prophet Muhammad (Pbuh) had to say about women:

A man came to the Prophet (Pbuh) and said, "O Messenger of God! Who among the people is the most worthy of my good companionship?" The Prophet (Pbuh) said: Your mother. The man said, "Then who?" The Prophet (Pbuh) said: Then your mother. The man further asked, "Then who?" The Prophet (Pbuh) said: Then your mother. The man asked again, "Then who?" The Prophet (Pbuh) said: Then your father.

This Hadith showed the reverence and respect that the Prophet Muhammad (Pbuh) had toward women.

There is another Hadith narrated by the Prophet Muhammad (Pbuh) that says:

"Your Heaven lies under the feet of your mother."

The meaning is that Paradise awaits those who cherish and respect their mothers.

At the conclusion of the lecture, the sisters of the Christian community had a totally different perspective of women in Islam. Contrary to what most of them had heard from other Christians or had seen portrayed in the media, they now realized that Muslim women were the backbone of

Muslim societies, and that they played a vital role in the development of our children and maintaining our households. They have also gained a great deal of respect and appreciation for the way that Muslim women dressed. I thanked the Christian sisters again for allowing me the opportunity to present this aspect of our faith and I admired them for venturing out of their comfort zone to learn about our remarkable sisters.

A month later, I was asked to conduct another lecture on Women in Islam for the University of Maryland (Asia Division). I was accompanied by our Muslim Chaplain's wife and one of the brothers from the Muslim community. That lecture also went well and was well appreciated by those who attended.

Another notable misconception about women in Islam is that Muslim women were not supposed to be educated. This was very far from the truth and much of it was propagated by the Taliban era in Afghanistan. Islamically, Muslim women have the same educational opportunities that the men have, but their priorities are the children and domestic responsibilities. Culturally, in many countries, women are deprived of their education. With my affiliation with Muslim countries, I've seen both ends of the spectrum. I've seen female Muslim lawyers, doctors, and engineers, and I've seen female Muslims that hadn't been given the opportunity to attend grade school. With the numbers of educated Muslim women in our society and abroad today, I am confident that the notion that Muslim women are not supposed to be educated can be dispelled.

Discrimination 101

In 2000, while stationed in Okinawa, Japan, I attended the Advanced Staff Noncommissioned Officer's Course as part of my Professional Military Education (PME) curriculum. When you reach the rank of Gunnery Sergeant, you're required to attend this school if in the future you wanted to be considered for the next rank of First Sergeant or Master Sergeant. The first training day of this school, just like every other formal Marine Corps school, starts off with a physical fitness test. In the warm months, our physical fitness uniform was green shorts and a green t-shirt. Muslims are not allowed to wear these shorts, unless they fall below your knees, so whether hot or cold I always wore green sweatpants over my shorts. Muslim males, when out in public are required to be covered from their navel to their knees and the standard Marine shorts were short and didn't go down that far. Knowing that the fitness test was the next day, I immediately went to my Squad Advisor to see if it was permissible to wear the sweatpants over my shorts. I went to my Squad Advisor's office and explained my situation. He said that he would have to run it through his supervisor for approval. He returned in a few minutes and said that it would be alright for me to wear the sweat pants over my shorts.

The next morning the students gathered to take the physical fitness test. While our instructors were ensuring accountability, the Deputy Director of the academy looked over at me and motioned for me to come to him. I walked over to him and the first thing he asked, was why I wasn't in the proper uniform. I replied that I was a Muslim and that Muslims couldn't wear shorts that rested above their knees. He asked if I had shorts under my sweatpants and I told him that I did. He then told me to go inside, take the sweatpants off, and the next issue that came up about my religion, would have me dropped from the course. I was not pleased with what he told me to do but I did it because I didn't want to take a chance in getting dropped from the course. This course was the gateway to my next promotion and I didn't want to jeopardize that. I felt that I was being discriminated against and I felt helpless because I didn't know who to turn to. This was the first time that I had been discriminated against since I became Muslim in 1994. Why should I have to compromise my religion for something as small as wearing sweatpants over my shorts? I decided to leave the issue alone until after graduation. That way, if conflict was generated from the incident, I would already have my completion certificate in hand and there would be nothing that they could do to me. I continued wearing the shorts for the duration of the course, meanwhile thinking of a way to present the discrimination issue to the leadership of the academy.

About three days before graduation, the Director of the academy asked the class in forum if anyone had any issues during the course that needed to be brought to his attention. I felt that this was my opportunity to address the issue. Directly after the forum I went to the Director's office to explain what happened. He listened to my story and firmly stated that the actions of the Deputy Director were wrong. He also stated that he would talk with the Deputy and asked if I would go back and talk with him after he did. The next day I returned to the Deputy's office to hear what he had to say about the issue. I told him that the Director asked me to talk with him to see if we could put some closure to what had happened.

My thinking was that the Director sent me to his office to get an apology from the Deputy.

The first thing he uttered was that he was A.M.E. (African Methodist Episcopal) and that he didn't think that he said or did anything wrong. Seeing that he outranked me by two pay grades, there wasn't too much I could say. I could threaten him about going to the Base Equal Opportunity Advisor, but how far would they take it? In 2000, I wasn't familiar with the equal opportunity process so I didn't have confidence in the system. I figured that I would just deal with my religious issues as they came and not create waves that would make Muslims sound like they were not conforming to Marine Corps policy. To my knowledge, there was no policy that stated when you came out for physical fitness at a formal school in the Marine Corps, you can't wear green sweatpants over your green shorts, regardless of what is required by your religious preference. I really felt that I was wasting my time in his office looking for an apology, so I told him good afternoon, did an about face, and left his office.

Walking back to my barracks, I seriously contemplated talking to the Equal Opportunity Advisor. I thought to myself that it would probably be a lot of paperwork for nothing. The thought also crossed my mind that if I didn't address the issue with the Equal Opportunity Advisor, how was that going to help the next Muslim that came through the academy? The fact that I faced religious discrimination at a formal Marine Corps school really bothered me. I could see something like this happening ten years ago but not in the year 2000. I graduated two days later and decided not to pursue the issue. In retrospect, I should have reported it.

Religious Tolerance

Approximately six months after the academy issue, one of the Muslim brothers in the community approached me and said that he was being discriminated against at his workplace. He was working as a Motor Transport Driver and his supervisor refused to let him pray in the motor pool. He asked if he could pray in the corner when they told him that there wasn't enough space in the motor pool. When he found space to pray, his supervisor then said that it wasn't safe for him to pray there. They also said that it took too long to pray, and that time could've been utilized for work production. Knowing that it only took a few minutes to conduct his prayers, he asked his supervisor about the Marines that took between seven to ten minute cigarette breaks a day. His supervisor ignored him. The brother had mentioned to me a few weeks earlier that his office didn't accept him as a real Muslim because he was Caucasian. Anyone that knows a little about Islam realizes that there are millions of white Muslims. This was just another case where the Marine Corps had failed to properly train their personnel on Islamic culture and religious tolerance.

Serving in the capacity as the Islamic Lay Leader, I suggested that we talk to his unit Chaplain, Equal Opportunity Advisor, Sergeant Major and Commanding Officer. I called his Chaplain to arrange a meeting, and the next day we met in their conference room to see if we could educate the leaders of this command on Islam and convince them to implement religious tolerance for not only Muslims but for all faith groups. The meeting was a success and the brother was allowed to pray at the motor pool.

After the outcome of the meeting, I thought about the academy issue and wondered what would've happened if I had gone to the Equal Opportunity Advisor. That was definitely a lesson learned for me. The Equal Opportunity Advisor for the academy was in the same chain of command as the Advisor for my brother. If they had conducted classes on Islam and religious tolerance six months earlier from that issue, this issue might've never occurred. Allah knows best.

Air Force Muslim Chaplain

In June of 2001, my oldest daughter decided to join the Air Force after graduating from high school. She tested and took the physical but at that time the Air Force could not guarantee her the job she wanted, which was Laboratory Technician. She told her recruiter that she would enlist when the Air Force could guarantee her the job she wanted. In October of the same year, she received a call from her recruiter informing her that her job was guaranteed. She enlisted and was scheduled to leave for boot camp at Lackland Air Force Base, San Antonio, Texas in December of that year. Before she departed I asked her to keep me informed of her graduation date because I would try to make it to her graduation.

We heard from her a few times while she was at boot camp and she relayed the graduation date. I booked a reservation for the flight out of Okinawa. It would be a long flight but it would be well worth it. I called my mother in Virginia to see if she wanted to attend the graduation. This would be my first time in San Antonio, Texas, the city that I had heard so much about.

I arrived in San Antonio two days before the graduation and my mother was due in the next day. I picked up a rental car and drove to the base to find billeting. Billeting was booked so I went off base to secure a room for my mother and myself. Next, I drove around to familiarize myself with the area. San Antonio was pretty simple to navigate. The two loops covered a very large portion of the city. My daughter had base liberty that next day so I was able to meet her at the Reception Center where all of the families gathered.

After the Reception Center, she took me over to her flight barracks to show me their living quarters while at basic training. There she introduced me to some of the favorites in her flight and her Training Instructors or TIs. They each spoke highly about her. We then went to the Chapel to meet the Chaplain.

After I became Muslim, and later after my wife became Muslim, we began talking to our kids about Islam. We explained to them the differences between Christianity and Islam and the reasons why we decided to change our faith to Islam. We realized that we shouldn't force them to be Muslims and according to the faith, we couldn't because the Quran taught us that there is no compulsion in Islam. We felt that if we forced them then they wouldn't be good Muslims, just like we had seen in other faiths. We just asked them to keep an open mind and if they chose to be Muslims, fine, and if they didn't it was fine also. We also asked them to use us as examples and whenever they observed us not setting a good example to let us know. Every now and then we would ask them if they were ready to take their Shahadahs (Declaration of Faith) to become Muslims, just to see what they would say.

While my daughter was at boot camp, she heard that the base offered Islamic services on Sundays. She attended service that coming Sunday and surprisingly took her Shahadah. She called us the first opportunity she had to let us know. She even said that they had a Muslim Military Chaplain on the base. This came as a real surprise. At that time, I knew of two Muslim Navy Chaplains and two Muslim Army Chaplains, but I knew of none in the Air Force. I asked her to give him my greetings and to tell him that I would meet him when I came to San Antonio for her graduation.

This was our reason for going to the Chapel. We walked into his office and she introduced us. She went to the Muslim Prayer Room while we chatted. He was Caucasian and was originally from England. He had a very interesting story about how he came to Islam and furthermore why he chose to be a Muslim Chaplain. He was a Captain and I can't recall how many years he had served in the Air Force, nor could I remember how long he had been in the United States. He told me about the local masjid that he attended and he offered to take me while I was in town. He took me down the hall to see the Muslim Prayer Room. There were a few other Airmen there who my daughter had met while attending service. The Chaplain told me that he stayed pretty busy there.

Contrary to what most people might think, each Chaplain is a Chaplain for all faith groups. He was the Chaplain for each faith group that the Armed Forces recognized as a religion. Not only was he the Chaplain for the Airmen attending boot camp but the permanent personnel on the installation as well. We stayed at the prayer room for about an hour.

Next my daughter showed me where most of their training took place and she took me to the Marine Detachment that resides aboard the base. The Marine Corps Military Police Dog School was there and I just wanted to go in to talk to a few of the Marines. After our visit I dropped my daughter off at the Reception Center and I left to pick up my mother from the airport. Her plane was on time so we were in and out of the airport, grabbed a bite to eat and then went to the hotel room. I told her that I had spent about half of the day with my daughter. She looked forward to seeing her at graduation. She hadn't seen her in over a year.

The next morning we were out for the graduation. We picked a seat close to my daughter's graduating flight. They had a very nice graduation ceremony and afterwards she introduced more of her flight members to my mother and me. We chatted about thirty minutes and then we took my mother to downtown San Antonio to the River Walk and the River Center Mall. We toured most of the day until it was time to take my daughter back to her flight. We would not see her again because we had flights out the next morning. My daughter stayed in Texas for laboratory training and later traveled to Travis Air Force Base, California for her specialty training.

Overall, it was a wonderful trip. I got the chance to see my mother again who I hadn't seen in over a year. We had the chance to see my daughter graduate from boot camp, and I had the chance to meet the Muslim Chaplain that administered the Shahadah for my daughter to become Muslim. She felt that this was the time in her life when she needed new direction, spiritual guidance and the opportunity to start a new life based on solid principles, nothing ambiguous, discipline and serving to do the will of God. From that period forward, she made tremendous accomplishments and continued to excel in all of her endeavors. May Allah (swt) guide and keep her, Ameen.

September 11, 2001

9/11 was a day that affected all of mankind to the extent that we cannot let our guard down to the cowardly forces that would take innocent lives to try to justify their ideology of a faith that prohibited that type of behavior. The damage to those who lost lives in this tragedy cannot be repaired and the mental affects of our society would later lead to more hate and discontent.

I recall that morning in Okinawa when my wife and I were awaken by a call from her mother and she asked us to turn on the television. As we watched the first aircraft fly into the World Trade Center, we actually had to make sure that we weren't dreaming. We then thought that it was some type of sick movie that was being previewed. When we finally realized what had happened, we became numb. We couldn't move nor could we speak. I couldn't believe that anyone would have the nerve to come on American soil and deface our nation like that.

As we watched, we saw the second aircraft fly into the second building. We watched the debris fall from the building to the streets of New York. We watched people jump from the windows of the World Trade Center trying to escape the flames of the crash. We saw the streets of New York City in utter chaos.

As we watched on I was praying to myself that this was not an act of some extremist terrorist group, but as the morning went on we learned that Al-Qaeda was responsible for that senseless act of cowardice. I couldn't help thinking about the type of impact this catastrophe would have on innocent Muslims worldwide. The backlash from this incident was extremely difficult for the Muslims to overcome.

Soon after the tragedy took place, we started hearing stories about Muslims being physically assaulted on the streets and rocks and other debris being thrown through the windows of masjids and Islamic Centers. There were also reports of attacks on Sikhs who weren't Muslims but since they wore beards and turbans, they were mistakenly identified as Muslims. They also received threats of fire bombing. Many Islamic structures had to post 24-hour guards to deter angry citizens from committing these acts.

In addition to the physical retribution Muslims started to receive, there were also countless incidents of prejudice and discrimination aimed at Muslims. I can honestly say that our military community on the bases of Okinawa, Japan did not receive any threats or any acts of retribution from our military comrades. There were Unit Commanders that summoned their people of the Islamic faith and told them to report any incidents of discrimination, prejudice or verbal abuse to their chains of command.

In response to the terrorist attack, each base on Okinawa had to institute tougher security measures at their entry points. They restricted citizens from certain countries from entering the bases, such as those from Saudi Arabia, Yemen, and Pakistan. This affected my plans because I often brought the students from the Okinawa International Center (OIC) and University of the Ryukyus to the base for tours and shopping and some of them were from these countries mentioned. Prior to the attack, all that was required was their OIC Identification Card and their passports for entry. Now I was faced with bringing some students and leaving others, and I didn't want to put myself in that situation. It really didn't matter the next two months because the three Muslim communities lost touch with each other. All three communities were so emotionally stricken by the attack that hardly any of us had the desire to talk about it. It seemed like our lines of communication had totally shut down.

Within the military community the same pattern was noticed. We were not communicating like we were prior to the attack. Prior to the attacks, we sat around in circles and talked about issues and community projects that we felt would help the local community as well as our Muslim brothers and sisters living in countries deprived of the basic necessities like food, water, clothing, and shelter. After the attack on New York and the other two locations, activities after service halted. Everyone would either go back to work or go home.

Aside from all the negative, something positive happened after the attack. The tragedy brought our nation together. Whatever differences people had with each other, they were set aside while the nation focused on rescue efforts for those who were unfortunate enough to be in and in the vicinity of the Trade Center buildings. We witnessed firemen, policemen, paramedics, servicemen and regular citizens come from across the nation to give whatever assistance they could to help. We saw Christians, Muslims, Jews and other faith groups holding vigils to pray for those who lost loved ones, and peace for our nation. I really feel that it is a shame that the only time our nation pulls together is when tragedy strikes.

The attack also brought worldwide curiosity about Islam. The attack prompted many people to start researching about Islam to see what generated the people to commit such a heinous act against humanity. Fortunately, after researching, many were convinced that this was not the teaching and principles of Islam. They realized that the way the media portrayed this belief system was totally contradictory to what they had learned. Prior to the attack, many had no idea as to what the religion of Islam was about. Many searched for sources other than their friends and the media who had no desire to give them factual information about Islam. We learned that people went to Islamic websites on the internet and that churches and synagogues asked the Islamic leaders to present lectures to their congregations about Islam. We also found that stores and libraries could not keep enough Qurans on their shelves because of the overwhelming demand for the first hand knowledge about Islam.

One week after the attack, I went to our musallah for Friday service. The Chapel staff had unlocked the door before I arrived. I walked in and there was a gentleman standing inside. I greeted him and asked what I could do for him. He asked me how he could become Muslim. I asked him if he was sure about that and he replied, “Yes.” I told him that at that time Muslims were really being persecuted from the attack that happened in New York and he said that he knew it.

I then asked him why he desired to become Muslim. He told me that he had been researching the religion and had gained the real understanding about what Islam was all about. I asked him to sit through the service and to see if he had any questions. When the rest of the community arrived, I informed them that the gentleman had the desire to become Muslim. They all had the same puzzled look that I had, knowing what had just happened a week ago. After service we recommended that he wait about a week before taking his shahadah to become Muslim, just in case he had second thoughts. He said that he would come back the next Friday to accept Islam as his way of life. That next Friday he returned to do so, and a week later he wanted to officially change his name to a Muslim name.

About two months after the attack, we started hearing about scores of people with the desire to become Muslims. This was occurring all over the world, not just in the United States. It was noted that after 9/11, more people became Muslims than any other time in American history. It was also noted that during Operation Desert Storm in 1991, over one-thousand service members became Muslims during the one month long war and the five months of redeployment back to the United States. The majority of the reverts were Caucasian women. Many asked why that happened. Once people know the truth about true Islam, its teachings and principles, they're attracted to it. There is no blind faith following in Islam and there is no ambiguity. I've learned that those are two of the issues that Christians have with Christianity. Many Christians have learned like I did that the Muslims follow the teachings of Jesus (Pbuh) better than the Christians did. When you go to a Muslim country, you're exposed to it and what better way can you learn about a way of life other than living it or seeing it for yourself? They also failed to realize that we had an entire chapter about Jesus (Pbuh) and Mary in the Quran.

9/11 was devastating for our nation and it taught us a valuable lesson. As a nation that's involved in the political affairs of so many countries, we must remain vigilant of our shores, ports, borders, and air space. We the people of the United States must also elect government officials that represent our country well and that have no hidden agendas that cater to groups with special interests that are not beneficial to the American people. Furthermore, we should hold our President and his constituents accountable to ensure that organizations like the CIA and FBI operate under strict guidelines that uphold the highest standards of righteousness, morals and dignity. Lastly, the world should put its brightest minds together to find a solution to stop the genocide and land stealing in Palestine. I feel that much of the hatred toward the United States is generated from the atrocities and injustices that have taken place there.

Persian Carpets (The Best in the World)

If I took the alternate route on my way to work, I would pass by the Persian Carpet Shop right outside the Futenma Housing Gate. I told myself that I would stop in one day to meet the owner and possibly purchase one of the carpets that I had heard so much about. Eventually I stopped in after work. When I walked in, there was a small space at the door to leave your shoes. The rest of the space inside was covered with carpets piled about three feet high. A large amount of the wall space was covered by carpets also. The owner sat in the back of the store behind a partition usually drinking tea. As the bell rang when I opened the door, he stepped from behind the partition and welcomed me to his store. I told him that I was Muslim and he gave me the Islamic greeting. I knew that most Persian carpet shops were owned by Muslims.

He was a very delightful man from Pakistan in his sixties. Married to a Japanese National, he had lived in Okinawa for about seventeen years and carpets were his life and livelihood. They had two daughters who were in their teens. He spoke Urdu, Farsi, a little Pashto, and Japanese which came in handy as his imported carpet business weighed heavily on his ability to talk to import businessmen from four different countries to maintain a steady supply of carpets. Twice a year he traveled to Iran, Afghanistan, India and his native Pakistan to select some of the finest carpets in the world to bring to the Far East island of Okinawa. Although each country took pride in their carpet industry, Iran had been noted to have the finest hand woven carpets in the world, and once I sat down with him while he explained their technique, it made perfectly good sense as to why. From what I learned about the different styles of carpets that came from different areas of the four countries, each carpet told a different story in its own pattern and colors. Most intriguing was the process of mixing dyes and wools and having them sit in the sun for special colors. The owner had a wide assortment of colors, sizes, and textures and each piece was affixed with a label of authenticity. The owner guaranteed a life of 20 to 25 years per carpet if they were not placed in high traffic areas. The prices ranged from $250.00 to $15,000.00. Some of his most expensive carpets were stretched out across the walls with lights surrounding in order to display the portions of silk that were woven into their patterns. The lights from certain angles brought out the cultural beauty of the carpets. He rolled back several carpets that he thought that I would be interested in.

We went through four stacks of carpets before I noticed one that caught my interest. It was a beige 8' X 11' carpet from Isfahan, Iran. I knew that my wife would love this color because it would match the décor of our future home. I decided to go home to bring my wife back for her approval of the carpet. She too was in awe when she walked into the showroom. The first items she noticed were the expensive carpets hanging on the back wall with the lights beaming from different angles. After flipping through two stacks of carpets, I showed her the carpet I was interested in and she loved it. We asked the brother for the price and he told us that it was $2500.00, but he would let us have it for $1500.00. I asked about a payment plan and he told me to take the carpet home and pay him when I could. I'm not sure if he offered this because we were Muslims or if he just needed the business, but it suited us just fine.

My plan was to drop in about every two weeks with a payment and sit down with him to discuss what was going on in the Muslim world. He could speak intelligently on global current events so I was able to pick his brain about countries like Iran, Libya, and Sudan that most Americans did not understand. He also kept me abreast on the political situation in Pakistan, which was always discussed in the media. Just as Muslims do when making a business transaction, we wrote a contract and we both signed it for legitimacy. We took the carpet home but kept it rolled up until we returned to the states where we displayed it in our new home.

"Owner of the Persian Carpet Store in Okinawa, Japan."

Chapter Five

ORDERS HOME TO NORFOLK, VIRGINIA

Don't Hold it Against Me

My assignment to Marine Forces Atlantic, Norfolk, Virginia in 2005, was my second assignment at that headquarters. The headquarters was located in a secured compound off of Hampton Boulevard and was only accessible by three gates. The majority of the time I utilized the gate off of Hampton Boulevard because there was less traffic and I had developed a friendly relationship with one of the security guards that monitored the gate. During the course of my day, I would frequent the gate three to four times and most of the time, depending on his shift, he would be there. As I was waved through, I would always ask how he and his family were doing, as well as any other guard that were posted with him. I looked forward to greeting him, and honestly I feel that he felt the same way. One afternoon I approached the gate as he was standing there with his co-worker. He smiled as I was driving up and he motioned for me to stop my vehicle. He walked to my window and explained to his co-worker that I was always in good spirits, always had a smile on my face, and that I gave everyone the utmost respect. His co-worker replied that she noticed it and stated that I must be living right. My friend then asked what church I attended. He assumed that since I displayed good personal attributes, I had to be affiliated with a good church. I replied that I didn't attend any church because I was

Muslim. Stunned by my reply, he looked at his co-worker, glanced back at me and his whole demeanor changed. His reply to me was, "Oh, I knew that there was something different about you." From that day forth, we didn't have the same relationship, and the fact that I was a Muslim was the reason why. I was hurt and disappointed and they both could see it on my face. He waved me through the gate and I told them to have a good day. After that conversation, when I drove through the gate, I basically just received a wave through and a "How are you," without even a smile.

Always conscientious because I'm Muslim, I always made it a point to exemplify good character and morals whenever I came into contact with people. I couldn't understand why the guard didn't see me as the same person that was cordial, respectful and in good spirits all the time. Was his dislike for Muslims that strong to risk losing a meaningful relationship? I considered myself a good Muslim and Muslims deserve the right to exist in this country just like any other faith group. Don't hold the fact that I'm a Muslim against me.

Resisting the Taliban

Five months after arriving to the Tidewater area, one of the brothers told me about a brother who had just arrived in the area. He told me that the brother was from Afghanistan and that he had an interesting story. The brother lived in Newport News not far from my mother's home. I wrote down his number for the next time I would visit my mother. When I did visit my mother again, I called him to see if I could come meet him. When I met him, I was a bit stunned. The brother was a double amputee. He was missing both legs from the knees down. He asked me to sit down and he went on to explain his misfortune. The town that he was from in Afghanistan was under tight rule of the Taliban regime. He realized that the only way that the country could rid itself of the Taliban was to help the Americans against them, so he drove vehicles for the Army Special Forces. He knew the area well and he had resources that could inform allied forces of their whereabouts. The brother spoke four languages and because of this advantage, he was an invaluable asset to the Special Forces.

While out with the Forces on a mission, his truck ignited a roadside bomb and he and his comrades were blown into the air. He was knocked unconscious and the next time he woke up, he was being treated at a hospital in Germany. He realized then that he had lost both legs from the knees down. Because of the injury, he lost more blood than he could afford to lose so he was fighting for his life. He managed to make it through multiple surgeries and was taken out of critical status. He remained in the hospital for months until he was flown to Walter Reed Army Medical Center in Washington, D.C., where most of the amputees are sent for counseling and prosthesis.

At the time we met, he was in a wheelchair. I asked if he was making progress with his prosthesis and he told me he wasn't because they hurt his legs. I even saw him maneuver out of his wheelchair a couple of times and utilized his arms to get around his apartment on the floor. He had gotten pretty good at getting around. He actually prayed next to me at prayer time. I asked which masjid he attended and he told me that he stopped going because the little boys there laughed at him when they saw him crawling at the masjid. He had gotten out of his wheelchair so that he could prostrate on the floor.

I then asked him how he managed to come to Virginia. He told me that the Army, through the State Department had a Christian group sponsor him there in the area. Once he told me that, I knew what was coming next. He said that the group financially supported him until he started to receive public assistance. In the meantime, Immigration was working on his American citizenship. He was a special case so his citizenship was being expedited. While the Christian group financially supported him, they would drop by to visit and bring him Bibles and Christian literature with intentions of converting him to Christianity. He said they were very nice and they always treated him with the utmost respect. He even kept their Bibles and literature in his drawer. I had seen this same scenario over and over again when Muslims from third world countries come to the United States. He told me that he had no intentions of converting to Christianity but he always took time to sit and talk with them when they dropped by.

I asked if he had children and he told me that he had five. He told me that his wife and children moved in with his father for protection after his ordeal. He had only talked with them once since the accident. He pulled out his wallet and showed me three of his children and told me their names. The only possessions he had of his family were those three photos. His wallet was his only possession when his truck hit the roadside bomb. Because of his condition, he didn't get to go back to see his family. He told me that once he received his citizenship, he could send for them. I asked if he would go back to Afghanistan and he told me that he couldn't because the Taliban would kill him. He mentioned that they had already gone to his father's house looking for him.

As we talked, he expressed how proud he was to work with the U.S. Army Special Forces. The Taliban had made life in Afghanistan so miserable, that he was elated to do what he could to help exterminate them. He told me that the Army had given him an award for his heroism and I asked to see it. He proudly took it off the wall and gave it to me. My eyes got full of tears when I saw what the Army had given him. It was a copy of a copy of a "Letter of Appreciation." There were only three lines on the award and I recall reading, "Thank You for Your Service" at the end. It looked like the award was given to someone else; they made a copy of it and changed the name to his. I could not believe that this was all they gave him for his contributions. He was so proud of it that he framed it. I could only imagine what type of award he should have gotten for his sacrifices. He placed the award back on his wall, smiling.

I kept in contact with the brother by email and by phone and whenever I came to my mother's, I went by to see him. My wife and I invited him to our house for dinner one day so he was able to meet my family. The local newspaper did an article on him one day and they had a full page to show his picture and to tell his story. He had learned to ride the bus system and once the driver started talking with him, he realized how interesting his story was. A few weeks after the story was printed, he was hired at the local Immigration Office as a translator.

Fortunately, I was present at the ceremony when he was sworn in for his U. S. Citizenship. What a proud moment that was for him. He had also invited his Afghan friends and members of the Christian group that sponsored him when he first arrived. After I left the area with orders to Japan, he was hired for a job in Orlando, Florida where they made prosthesis. I lost contact with him at that time.

It was a pleasure knowing this brother. I felt honored every time that I told someone about his story. In my eyes he was a hero. To make it through the adversity that he faced took a great deal of courage and suffering and yet he had a heart of gold. I made it my duty to try and locate him after I wrote this portion of my book. You'll know in one of the later chapters if I was able to do so.

From the Pulpit to the Mimbar

While stationed in Norfolk, Virginia in 2003, I attended the Islamic Center of Tidewater on the campus of Old Dominion University. The university maintained a large contingency of Arab, African, and Pakistani Muslims, majoring in fields from Physical Education to Computer Science. I've had many conversations with a number of them who had a great deal of respect for the school and its administration that had gone out of their way to accommodate the Muslims culturally and religiously. Hate crimes started to occur after 9/11, but the administration made a commitment to prosecute anyone that was caught committing a hate crime against the Muslims or vandalizing the masjid. There was a case where bricks were thrown through the windows of the masjid late one night. Although the culprits were never caught, the masjid went on with business as usual and didn't post twenty-four hour guards, unlike many other masjids did as a deterrent.

After Friday prayers one particular Friday, the Imam announced that we would be having a special guest coming in for the weekend. The guest would be a former Protestant Christian preacher from Texas, who had reverted to Islam. He was also a devout member of the group "The Disciples of Christ." As mentioned in a previous chapter, I say reverted because everyone is born a Muslim, submitting to do the will of God, but it's their parents that change them to Christians, Jews, etc. It was not uncommon for Christian priests and preachers to accept Islam. It had been happening at a rapid rate. Once people were exposed to the true teachings of Islam, it automatically attracted them. This was evident by a debate that was held in Sudan years ago between Christian and Muslim scholars. The goals of the debate were to first compare the Bible and Quran for authenticity and then to compare the practices of the two religions. Five Christian scholars debated against five Islamic scholars. At the end of the debate, four out of the five of the Christian scholars accepted Islam as their way of life. There were countless debates with the same results.

That Saturday morning after the Fajr prayer, we met with him and he began to tell us about his reversion to Islam. His father, who was a Reverend, had business dealings with an Egyptian man, who they asked to reside with them for a while. His presence led to many discussions about religion. Those discussions resulted in his reversion to Islam, along with his wife, his father, and a homeless suicidal Catholic Priest that the family took in from a homeless shelter. He mentioned that his real intentions were to convert the Egyptian man to Christianity. His newfound knowledge of Islam forced him to re-evaluate his beliefs on Christianity, especially the concept of the Trinity, which was considered the foundation of Christianity. What many Christians failed to realize was that the validity of the Trinity was voted on by the Council of Nicea in 325 A.D. That, and other critical facts about Christianity convinced him that he and most other Christians were not following the true teachings of Jesus (Pbuh), and that the teachings of Islam were more comparable to what Jesus (Pbuh) taught. This is what took him from the pulpit to the mimbar. A mimbar is the area of the masjid where the khatib gives the khutbah. It is very similar to the pulpit where a minister gives his sermon.

After he told us the story about the reversion of himself and his family, he dialed up on his laptop and went live on his website; islamtomorrow.com. His website gave you the entire story about his conversion. From there he answered questions from those who dialed in and we were able to hear their conversations. He fielded a wide range of questions from people of various religious backgrounds. He stayed on the air for about thirty minutes and then he had a question and answer period for those who attended the lecture. There were curious Christians and Jews in the audience. After he answered the audience's questions, he was shuttled over to another masjid for much of the same routine. The audience that gathered at the masjid that morning was really intrigued by his story and his knowledge on an array of Islamic topics.

After the brother's reversion to Islam, he pursued the Arabic language and focused on Quranic studies in Turkey, Egypt, and Morocco. In 1994, he was named the National Chaplain for the U. S. Bureau of Prisons and he was a delegate to the United Nations Peace Summit for Religious Leaders in 2000. He had established numerous hi-tech Islamic websites, including chat rooms, video conferencing, news sites, and reference sites. He continued to conduct speeches and interviews world-wide and was currently residing in Northern Virginia with his wife.

"Family photos in San Antonio."

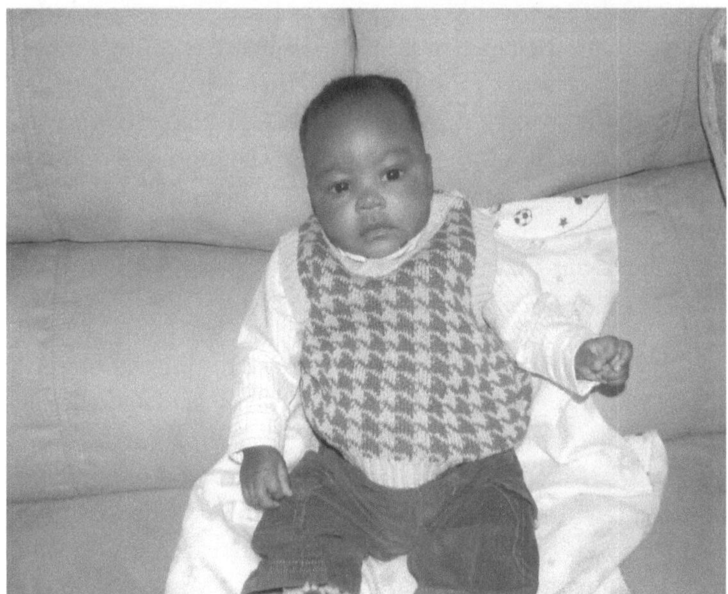

Grandson: Idris Naim Siddiq Camp, Born 30 August 2010

Chapter Six

RETURNING TO THE LAND OF SUNSHINE

Having the opportunity to go back to Okinawa in July of 2005 was a blessing. My wife had asked several times when we returned in 2002, if I ever thought that we would get the opportunity to go back. I told her that we didn't have a chance of going back because of my 2002 overseas control date that lets my monitor know that I had just returned from overseas. My monitor was the Marine at Headquarters that monitored my career path and gave all of my assignments. The monitors made decisions of duty preferences based on your rank and experience. Once an overseas assignment is completed, you usually are not assigned to another overseas assignment for about six years. This was not the case with me because my family and I had just returned three years prior.

When I returned from Japan in 2002, my Administration office never updated my overseas control date. Although they updated the rest of my record, strangely, the overseas control date was not adjusted. Needless to say, my record reflected that I hadn't been overseas in over ten years and my monitor wanted to ensure that I be assigned an overseas tour. That worked great for us because we loved being there and it gave us another three years to enjoy the Japanese culture. The only thing different was that we were returning without our two oldest children. My oldest daughter who was then in the Air Force was now stationed in San Antonio, Texas, and my son **Michel Andre' Camp**, was home in school at Old Dominion University.

I contacted some of my friends, along with some of the Muslim community to let them know that we were returning to Okinawa for another three years. We were definitely looking forward to reuniting with our old acquaintances. We would pick up where we left off in 2002 and enjoy more of the experiences that being in the Far East had to offer.

Ramadan 2006/Naha Okinawa Marathon

In June of 2006, while stationed in Okinawa, Japan, my command decided to form a running club to prepare for the Okinawa Marathon that was scheduled in December. Our Executive Officer and his wife, who were avid marathon runners, took the daunting task of putting together a running program that was geared to ensure that each runner of the club would successfully complete the 26.2 mile marathon. Once the word was spread about the club, we assembled about 15 dedicated runners that sacrificed their Saturday mornings for the mental and physical conditioning. Prior to our first run, they had some experts come to one of our runs to talk about running shoes, socks, hydration and running attire. The experts also gave us some good tips about water stops and race preparation that were beneficial on race day.

Having already run the Honolulu Marathon of Hawaii twice in 1994 and 1997, I wanted to set a goal of completing the marathon in 3 hours and 59 minutes. My two previous marathons were 4:13 and 4:17 respectively, and this was not with the training regimen that we would undergo in Okinawa. My desire was to keep my time below 4 hours. My motivation during my previous marathons came from watching the Kenyans in 1994 as they ran effortlessly along the 26.2 mile course, taking the top six positions at the tape. I saw them twice during the run, once at the start of the race before the gun and the second time was when I reached the 11 mile mark and they were all in stride heading back to the finish. They were bunched in a group and it looked as if they were barely breathing hard. I said to myself when I saw them, "There is no way that I'm not finishing this run." The winning time was 2 hours and 9 minutes. The next time that I saw the Kenyans was on the ten o'clock news that night where they showed them at the awards ceremony collecting their paychecks. The Kenyans had a long legacy of successful marathon runners, along with the Ethiopians and Mexicans. They traveled across the globe in the marathon circuit, and strategically chose the runs that they would do well in.

Training started in June and led us into December which was in the midst of Ramadan. I calculated that Ramadan would start three weeks before the marathon. I knew it would be a real challenge because Muslims can't eat or drink in the daylight hours during Ramadan. My running club members who knew I was Muslim repeatedly told me that they couldn't understand how I endured the physical exertion and heat without drink or food. I explained after the first time I heard it that I took fasting very seriously and that the spiritual and physical benefits of fasting are too beneficial to pass up. On another note, our doctrine told us that if you had conditions that were harmful to your health, refrain from fasting. As a distance runner, nutrition and hydration were paramount for peak performance.

Additionally, the summer months in Okinawa were brutal. The heat and humidity had caused many to have either heat stroke or heat exhaustion. Each member of the club donated money for bananas, oranges and Gatorade that would be staged along our run routes as we did our practice runs. Water was great for hydration but Gatorade replaced your electrolytes lost due to physical exertion. We started our first run with 8 miles and gradually increased to 10, 12, 14, and 18 miles. A week prior to the marathon we completed the half-marathon (13.1 miles), running the same course as we would actually run for the full marathon.

In addition to our long Saturday runs for endurance, individually I ran 4-6 miles twice a week. I kept it 4-6 miles to save energy for the Saturday runs. I did this prior to work before the Okinawa heat became unbearable. The key was all day hydration the day prior to every run. I utilized the days between runs to let my body recuperate and to combat soreness.

Our first 8 mile run went well. We had stagger starts with the slow runners starting 10 minutes ahead of the second group and so forth. That way, the faster runners would not have to wait too long for everyone to finish. We had water and Gatorade at the half-way point as well as the emergency vehicle in case runners were having difficulties. Although our first run went well, it was only a warm-up compared to a few of the runs that we had to look forward to.

It was during the 12 and 14 mile runs that I was fasting during Ramadan. The after-effects of these runs were extremely difficult because I had to endure the rest of the day until sunset without water or food. I had to break my fast after the 14 mile run because I felt light-headed and ready to faint. It was permissible to break the fast but if we did so, we have to feed a poor person or donate money to charity, and make up the fasting day at the conclusion of Ramadan. After hydrating I went home to lie down until I regained my strength. That was the first time that I had ever felt like that after a run.

When we first started talk about a running club, we decided that we would purchase shirts for the club. The best place to have the shirts made was in Korea where most teams were having their uniforms and sweat-suits made. Since I knew a few of the vendors in Korea, I volunteered to make the trip. I figured that while I was there, I could shop for other items as well. I spent a week in Korea and on my first day there, I presented our design to the vendor and he said that he could make the 15 shirts in about five days. I paid him up front and off I went to another vendor who specialized in making sweat-suits. Two of our team members wanted sweat-shirts to go with the shirts. Since our unit was Marine Wing Headquarters Squadron One, we chose "Team One" as our run club title. We included our unit logo and team name on the shirts.

The evening prior to race day we had to ensure that we loaded our bodies on carbohydrates to maximize our energy levels during the race. Pasta and spaghetti were our main sources. Gatorade and water were paramount also for hydration. We also spent much of the day prior just laying around relaxing to conserve energy.

The morning of race day, December 3rd, was filled with anxiety and anticipation. The moment had finally arrived where we would put all of our training to use. This was our test to see if our hard work and dedication would pay off. As we car-pooled the twenty minute ride down to Naha, the running tips and training constantly flashed across my mind. The running strategy that I obtained from the half-marathon would be utilized so I had to rethink that particular run. That course was filled with gradual hills that led me to a slow climb but I picked up the pace on the way down. For our half-marathon we started at the park at mile 13 so we didn't experience the layout of the first 13 miles. I figured that I would be alright because we trained well. Once arriving at the race site, we stretched and studied the diagram of the race layout. All runners were required to register on-line so we were mailed our numbers. The rest of the time prior to start time was spent staying loose and just enjoying the 30,000 runners that took the challenge.

Once we received the ten minute warning, we started working our way through the crowd to get as close as we could to the starting line. We managed to find a space about one hundred yards from the starting line. Once the gun went off we were at a walk until the runners up front started widening the gap.

The first leg of the run we ran through the shopping district of Naha City, recognizing many of the stores that we frequented. The second leg took us through the rural Okinawa villages and the third down to the park at the half-way point. The second half of the run was grueling. The heat combined with the hills started to take affect on many of the runners. I focused on grabbing a cup of water and a watered sponge at every three water stops. Spectators and volunteers lined both sides of the course from the start of the race so hydration was not a problem.

By this time I had split up from the group that I initially started the race with. The hills had caused a couple to fall back and another was experiencing cramps. I too had started to experience some pain in my knee but as I had done previously, I decided to just try and tough it out. The Okinawa Nationals were using a spray out of a can to relieve aches and pains. I asked the gentleman next to me if it actually worked and he said it did. I stopped, took a three second spray on my knee and started running again. Amazingly, the pain went away. At that point I was at mile 18 and I kept thinking that it was only a matter of time before the pain would come back. The pain never resurfaced.

At mile 20 as we headed over the bridge leading back into Naha City, I started to feel the sense of accomplishment. As the crowds of volunteers and spectators got larger, my determination and motivation increased immensely. I passed by the mile marker that read "6 Miles to Go" and I seemed to get a burst of energy out of the already drained body of mine. Mentally I pictured reaching the finish line and taking off my shoes to rest my feet. I was interrupted by the yelling of the on-lookers urging us to keep running.

As I ran further I could see the fence surrounding the Japanese Army base that was only three miles from the stadium finish line. I remembered that location from our 13 mile practice run. Only this time my body was a lot more fatigued. I wasn't that concerned because with only three miles left, I could finish the run on just adrenaline. I pushed on through the last leg of the run. Through a couple of side streets and the major intersection I could see the top of the stadium off in the distance. The runners at this point were picking up their pace utilizing the last bit of energy their body's could muster up to finish. We only had a quarter of a mile before we would enter the stadium. I looked behind me to see if I could find any of the runners from the run team. I wanted to cross the finish line with them but I couldn't find anyone within a forty to fifty yard radius.

As I entered the stadium, I only had a quarter-mile track to have completed my third marathon. The crowd cheered the runners on from each side of the stadium and I could see both rested and exhausted runners throughout the stadium. As I ran through the final shoot I stared at the time clock ahead to get a glimpse of my finish time. I finished with a time of 5 hours and 5 minutes. It was not the time that I was shooting for but under the circumstances I was alright with it.

After I crossed the finish line, the organizers led me into the line where I would tear off the scanned part of my number so that they could scan it for my race information. Then I went to the line where they issued medallions and t-shirts. I looked for the members of the run team that had finished prior to me. They were assembled in the stadium seats trying to replenish their bodies with liquids while snacking on fruits and energy bars. They congratulated me as I walked up and hurried to find a place to sit down to rest my aching legs and feet. I then watched as the other runners made their way around to the finish line. Slowly the rest of the run team joined us as they finished. Once the last team member completed the run, we took a group photo. I saw how much it pained everyone to move after we had gotten comfortable. Our muscles had stiffened up so we all walked like robots.

It was a tremendous feeling to accomplish yet another marathon. To put your body through a 26 mile physical challenge and succeed definitely deserved a pat on the back. For my teammates and me, six months before the marathon, it had been a dream. Finally, it became a reality. Life was about setting goals and achieving them. This was one that will hold a special place in my heart. The struggle from both Ramadan and the marathon strengthened my physical abilities and my discipline, while allowing me to adhere to one of the pillars of my faith.

"Eid Ul Fitr 2006 Prayer and Feast at Ryukyu University, Okinawa, Japan."

Muslims in Seoul, Korea

In March of 2007, I had the opportunity to go Temporary Additional Duty (TAD) for a month to Osan Air Force Base, Korea for a Joint Forces Exercise. It was great that the exercise was held in Korea because that's where the best shopping was and it gave me a chance to visit the masjid in Itaewon, Seoul. I heard that there was a masjid there but I had never been there. I was assigned with the Marine Liaison Detachment there at Osan and basically my job was to transport VIPs flying in for the exercise and directing Marines stopping through the Liaison Office. We were billeted in the Tent City on the west side of the base near the golf course. We pretty much worked regular work hours during the exercise unless we had VIPs arriving after hours.

The first opportunity that I had, I was headed for Seoul. The base had a shuttle that ran almost every hour to the Yongsan Army Base in Seoul for $4.50 one way. The trip took about an hour. I received a telephone number for a couple of the Air Force brothers that were there on the base so I called them to see if they cold make the trip with me. One couldn't make it but the other could, so we were off to the bus station. Fortunately, the brother had been to the masjid before so he knew how to get there. The bus dropped us off at the bus station on the Army Base and we took a taxi from there. I kept the route in my mind because the next time I would come, I'd probably walk to the masjid if it wasn't too far.

The taxi ride took about ten minutes and I memorized the route. We rode through the main shopping street and I remembered the landmarks. The street leading up to the masjid was lined with Muslim stores and it was obvious that we had entered the Muslim subdivision because of the way the people were dressed. They had halal meat stores, clothing stores and markets, all Muslim owned. Many of the Muslims had either purchased homes or were renting right there in the area where the masjid was. It was a fairly large masjid, equipped with its own Islamic school.

This was the Seoul Central Masjid, the largest of the nine masjids in South Korea. It was opened in 1976 and it had become a popular tourist attraction in Seoul. It had a multi-ethnic congregation of Arabs, Indians, Pakistanis, Turks, and Koreans. I saw a few American military members, but not many. I was really surprised at the number of Muslims that were there. After prayer we met and talked with a few brothers and then we left for lunch at the Turkish Restaurant next door. It was really convenient to have the restaurant so close. That would be my place to eat whenever I came to the masjid. We ate at the restaurant and the food was great. It would not bother me to eat Turkish food every day. After lunch we went back to the bus station to head back to Osan.

While shopping outside the gate at Osan one day, I came across a Persian carpet store with an owner who looked to be Pakistani. I entered the store to talk with him. I told him that I was in the military and that I would be there a few more weeks. He told me that he was Pakistani and that he and his brothers owned two Persian Carpet stores and a restaurant. One carpet store and the restaurant were in Seoul. He lived in Seoul but commuted to Osan every day to tend the store. He told me to let him know when I wanted to go to their restaurant, and he would call his brother so that I could eat free.

A week later I took him up on his offer. I went to his store and told him that I was going to Seoul that day to attend Friday prayers at the masjid. The restaurant was called "Usman's" and it was located right off of the main shopping street. When I arrived, the hostess was waiting for me. I sat down and ordered my favorite Pakistani foods, tandoori chicken, chicken masalla and naan. Their food was splendid also. Now I had two places that I could go for good food. Before I left I told his brother that I had to bring my wife there on our next vacation to Korea.

My thirty days on the exercise went pretty fast but I managed to see the brother a few more times and attend the masjid a few more times as well. Overall, Korea, although cold, was a good experience. Any opportunity that I got to pray in a different masjid and to meet new Muslims was a blessing. I'll always look forward to going back to Korea whether for business or pleasure.

"The Seoul Central Masjid in Seoul, Korea.
This is the largest of the nine Masjids in Korea."

Ramadan 2007

As Ramadan approached, we began preparing ourselves for the long vigorous days of fasting and the spiritual mindset that enabled us to maximize the benefits of Ramadan. Ramadan was not only about fasting but sacrifice, humbleness, and caring as well. Without these aspects, Ramadan was not fulfilled. Along with these aspects, prayers were increased and the sense of community was reinforced.

From conversations with the University Muslim community, there was a Tabligh Jammat coming from Mainland, Japan to spend about a week in Okinawa for Ramadan. A Tabligh Jammat is a group of Muslims who travel from place to place teaching about Islam and the beneficence and mercifulness of Allah (swt). These brothers were taking a twenty-four hour ferry ride over from the Mainland, where they were all involved in the used auto parts business. The University brothers picked them up and transported them from the Port of Naha, to the University.

After about three days at the University, they decided to come to Chatan for their remaining days on Okinawa. Chatan is the area close to the bases. This presented a problem because there were no arrangements made for their billeting. We couldn't billet them on the base because they didn't possess military identification cards, and the base would consider it a security concern. We began looking off base for a suitable place for them to stay. There were ten of them which made things extremely difficult.

We contacted one of the Muslim brothers who lived in Chatan to see if he could provide assistance. He was an Iranian who had been living in Okinawa for about fifteen years and he spoke fluent Japanese. He was also married to a wonderful Japanese National and at times he served as a translator for the Japanese Law Enforcement. He had gained the reputation of a successful businessman, selling cars at his own dealership. Once we contacted the brother, he informed us that the Japanese Law Enforcement had already contacted him about the visiting brothers and that they were on surveillance since they departed the ferry at Naha Port.

The search began for a place for them to stay and the brother already had a place in mind. He advised me to take them to a small house that the brother had used for guests visiting Okinawa. We walked to the house to see if it was suitable. If you could imagine ten foreigners and seven of them with beards, dressed like the Taliban, walking through the tiny streets of

Okinawa, you would've been scared to death. Each of the ten brothers, representing Sri Lanka, India, and Pakistan had full thick beards and they were dressed in their traditional shalwar khameeses. It was a sight that would stop anyone in their tracks if they had a slight inclination about the Taliban or anything that's going on in that geographical location of the world.

Although they were no threat to the security of the base, I couldn't take them aboard because they would draw too much attention. Upon entering the house, we realized that the house could only accommodate six of the brothers, so we asked the brother if he had another place in mind. He informed us that he had a friend who was out of town and had a vacant apartment. He called to see if it would be alright to accommodate our visitors. It was alright so we moved them in. They immediately began preparing food for Iftar that evening. I told them that I had to go home but I could return for Iftar and then Tarawee Prayers.

When I returned home, I called the brothers of the military community to let them know that the Tabligh Jammat was there and that they expressed the desire to see and talk with them about Islam and their spiritual goals. Before returning to the apartment with the Tabligh Jammat, I picked up one of the military brothers who wanted to meet them. When we walked into the apartment, we could smell the aroma of Pakistani food. The brothers had prepared chicken biryani for Iftar and we only had about forty-five minutes before breaking the fast.

When it was time to break the fast, we prayed the Maghrib prayer first and then ate Islamic style with one large dish of rice, meat, and bread placed in the center of a circle of men. The food was very tasty and we could tell that a couple of the brothers were experienced cooks of some sort. After we ate, we sat around in a circle and talked about stories of the Prophet Muhammad (Pbuh), the wives of the Prophet, the Sahabah, and hadith. Isha prayer quickly came upon us so we did that, along with Tarawee and then Witr prayers. The time spent with these brothers exemplified the true meaning of Ramadan. All of our conversations were pertaining to Allah (swt) or his Messenger (Pbuh) and sacrifices made for the Holy Month of Ramadan. We left the brothers that night looking forward to returning the next day for the same routine.

The next day the same brother and I came out to meet the brothers for Tarawee prayers. By the time we arrived, they had already finished dinner.

Again we prayed Maghrib and Isha prayers with them and then went into the Tarawee prayers. We left directly after the prayers because of work the next day but we had one more day to spend with them to soak up their knowledge and wisdom of the deen. Around mid-day of the following day, we received word that they had already left to return to the Mainland. I did manage to get a couple of phone numbers to stay in contact.

A week later we gathered at the University for the Eid Ul Fitr celebration which culminated the end of the month of Ramadan. I asked our two military Pakistani brothers why they didn't come out to meet the visiting brothers from their country. One replied that he was too tired after work and the other replied that he had a security clearance so he couldn't be seen with them by anyone in his command. I replied to him that I had a security clearance also and that I didn't feel the least bit threatened being seen with them. These were some of the most pious Muslims that I had ever met and just because they were from Pakistan, his native country, that didn't have strong ties with the United States, he was scared to be seen in public with them. I was devastated when I heard the brother say that. Maybe he felt that way because he was an Air Force Officer and that his command would think that he had ties to one of the militant groups through these brothers. I've seen this attitude displayed by Muslims before and some would even say that they are ashamed to be from their countries. If anything, they could have used a relationship with these brothers to try and bridge the gap of understanding between Pakistani Muslims and Muslims of the U. S. Military, which was so much needed in our unstable world today. Allah knows best.

Muslims in Bangkok, Thailand

In November of 2007, my wife and I decided to take our granddaughter on a trip to Thailand. We had heard so much about Thai culture and we wanted to experience it for ourselves. My command took part in a Joint Force Exercise there every year called Cobra Gold and the stories that the Marines would bring back would always leave me interested about Thailand. Thai food was always at the top of their list but my wife and I always wanted to ride on an elephant. Elephants are referred to as the "Beasts of Burden" and were very popular in Thailand. They were trained to do an array of tasks that range from farm work to logging. At one time in Thailand's history, they were even used in battle. We also wanted to experience the Floating Market in Thailand to see if it's actually like they say it was, and there we would try to haggle some bargains on the famous Thai gold.

I completed the security paperwork required by my command to travel to Thailand and my wife booked our reservations. A good friend of mine visited Thailand three months prior and he recommended a good hotel that many service members utilized when they go to Bangkok. We decided to book at the same hotel, the Somerset Suanplu, which was located in downtown Bangkok. He also recommended that same driver to pick us up from the airport and to serve as our tour guide. He called the gentleman and gave him our flight information.

We arrived in Bangkok and processed through immigrations. When we finished processing, there was a gentleman standing there with my name on his sign. We introduced ourselves and told him that he was highly recommended by my friend who had visited three months prior. The ride to the hotel took less than an hour. The driver told us about his family and how life was living in Thailand. He also revealed that he had a great deal of respect for Americans, especially their military. He dropped us off and we asked him to return in two days to take us on our tour. After checking in, we were told at the front desk that we flew in during the Thai holiday Loy Kratong, celebrating the completion of the rainy season. The celebration took place on the ninth floor at the pool area. We went up to see how they were celebrating. They had food, drinks, Thai dancers, and a free massage area, all lined up around the pool. My wife and granddaughter had a massage while we waited for the Thai dancers to perform. The people were very friendly and we met many of the staff that worked at the hotel.

Prior to leaving Okinawa, I called my Pakistani brother to let him know that the three of us were coming to Thailand. He and his brother, along with their wives who were sisters, ran an auto parts business there in Bangkok where they shipped containers full of auto parts to Pakistan and a couple of other countries. They had an apartment there in the city and a home in rural Bangkok. He told me to call once we arrived at the hotel. I met him a few months back while he was conducting the auto parts business in Okinawa.

We spent our next day in Bangkok sight-seeing and shopping. We started close to the hotel and then ventured out into the city. Clothing and jewelry were on our shopping lists and there was an abundance to choose from. We decided to have suits made at the tailor shop which we were measured for that day and the manager said that the suits would be brought to the hotel the day before we left. We couldn't find the gold bangles that my wife was looking for so we went back to the hotel for dinner. When we returned to the hotel there was a message at the front desk for me saying to call my Pakistani Brother. I gave him a call and he said that he was coming by the hotel to pick me up.

He arrived about an hour later on his moped. He gave me a helmet, I hopped on and off we were headed into downtown Bangkok. The traffic had really died down so that gave him the opportunity to open the throttle on the main streets and the back streets. He took me to their apartment to meet his brother. We had some chai tea and cookies as we talked. They operated their business from the bottom floor of their apartment. Their wives were at the family home in rural Bangkok.

Next he took me to a cyber café owned and operated by a Nigerian man. We talked about his business and how living was in Thailand. He had managed there for a few years and had liked it especially when you compared life there to his native country of Nigeria. He then took me to a masjid where the Muslims there were having dinner. He introduced me and they invited us to join them. I can never turn down Pakistani or Indian food. We all ate out of one large round dish full of rice, chicken and bread. I don't know what type of spices they used but they really blended well for a very tasty meal.

They had a lot of questions for me because I was an American Muslim. I didn't tell them that I was in the military. They were a mixed crowd of Indians and Pakistanis. I often heard about the animosity between the two groups because of the strip of land they're fighting for and have been fighting over for years called Kashmir. Both countries had lost many lives in an effort to gain control of the land. Of the Pakistanis and Indians that I have talked with, it seemed like there is only animosity between the two ethnic groups in that region. The fighting only existed there. After our conversation there, he took me to another masjid but we didn't go inside. He just wanted to show me the masjids that he attended. Now we were back on the moped on our way back to the hotel. He asked what we were doing the next day and I told him that the driver would pick us up for our tour. He said that he would pick us up in two days for more shopping and to meet the rest of his family.

The following morning our driver came by for us early and we told him what we had planned. We wanted to visit the famous Floating Market and we wanted to ride the elephants. He knew exactly where to go. We reached the elephant park and we could see tourists already riding elephants in different directions. We stood in line to get our tickets and when it was our turn to ride, we had to climb some stairs in a large tree and mount the elephant from a high platform. The three of us were scared getting into the seat because it was so high. As the elephant walked it really felt awkward because we swayed from side to side with every step. It took us about twenty-five yards to get adjusted to it, but it was an indescribable feeling. Although it seemed like we were riding slow, we were actually moving fast. The elephant even took us through about eight or nine feet of water and that was a little scary. The ride lasted about thirty minutes and the man that gave the elephant his commands, had the elephant lower him down so that he could take pictures of us. The elephant ride was a great experience.

From the elephant ride we went to the Elephant Zoo where my granddaughter posed with some baby elephants. She got a kick out of that. Next we were off to the Floating Market. The market was one of the most popular tourist attractions in Thailand. You actually rode through the market on little boats and when you saw something you like, you just asked the driver to stop the boat. You didn't even have to get out. We got out a couple times to reach some of the stores that were off the water. We were able to pick up some nice souvenirs. After the market we had the driver take us back to the hotel. The hour and a half ride gave us more opportunity to see more sights along the road. When we arrived at the hotel, we asked the driver to pick us up in two days to transport us back to the airport for our flight home. We ate Thai food at the hotel restaurant that evening.

The following morning my brother picked us up to take us to China Town. He said that China Town had the best gold prices. There my wife would look for her gold bangles. There were so many gold stores, it was hard to choose one. All of the prices were pretty much the same. My wife finally was able to get her Thai gold and it didn't hurt our pockets that much. When we left China Town, he took us to a park and a harbor cruise which was pretty fun. Later we left for their home in the rural countryside. The house was located about an hour outside of Bangkok in a town or province called Kukao Sansab Min Buri. He stopped about a mile from the house at his wife's aunt's house. He wanted to tell her to bring her daughter to the house to meet my granddaughter. I was really shocked when he told me that in about a two mile stretch on both sides of their house lives a Muslim community with clothing stores and markets. It was like a small Muslim city.

They had a beautiful home. Four families lived there, the parents of the three daughters, along with their husbands. Two of the sisters were there and we waited for the other and her husband to come. Their father was a retired Captain from the Royal Thai Air Force, and he was a very humble man. I asked him what he did for a living now and he told me that he worked in his garden and he went to the masjid. He actually prayed all five of the daily prayers at the masjid every day. The mother and sisters were preparing lunch for us when the third sister arrived. All three sisters looked so much alike it was hard to tell them apart, especially with their hijabs on. We ate shortly after the third sister, her husband, and cousin arrived. We ate all Thai cuisine and it was very good. They took some of the spice off because they knew that we weren't used to it. Regular Thai food is very spicy.

The clock sounded after lunch for prayer time so we washed up to go to the masjid. As we pulled into the parking lot of the Masjid Islam Makrez Tabligh, my brother showed me where they were building a new home. The house would be constructed directly behind the masjid. He showed me the floor plans and model of the house. The masjid had a Madrassa or Islamic School for boys. It might have been about 200 students there concentrating on Islamic studies. We all prayed together in one group and then we went back to the house.

We talked until the next prayer time and then we went to another masjid in the other direction. This one was not as large but it served the same purpose. We prayed there and went back to the house. We stayed about another hour and then headed back to the city. It was such a pleasure to spend the day with him and his family. I envied his father-in-law for the life style he lived there. Every day was so peaceful and stress free, I see why and how he felt so good living there. I pray that when I retire, I'll be able to reach that level of tranquility and spiritual peace. I told his father-in-law that I wanted to be just like him when I retired and he just smiled. My brother dropped us off and we thanked him for such a wonderful day with his family. We told him that we would definitely visit again on another vacation.

We were back on a plane the next morning for our return flight to Okinawa. We accomplished everything that we wanted to do in Thailand, and best of all we had the opportunity to meet and spend time with more wonderful Muslims. This would be another chapter in our lives that we would cherish and share with family and friends.

"Riding the famous elephants of Thailand."

With our Thai Family at their home in rural Bangkok

Between North and South Korea

While on an exercise in Korea in February 2008, the command put together a tour to the Demilitarized Zone (DMZ). The DMZ is a buffer zone between North and South Korea, that's 155 miles long and 2.5 miles wide. It's located at the 38th Parallel and it cut the Korean peninsula in half. I had heard the term during Marine Corps History classes but I never knew what it meant. At that time we were living at the Tent City at the Republic of Korea (ROK) Marine Camp near Osan, Air Force Base. When the First Sergeant announced the trip, I knew it would be the chance of a life time. I had heard so many stories from military members that had visited.

We went on a Saturday so that it would give everyone the opportunity to take advantage of the trip. We had four busloads of Marines taking part in the tour. First we were taken to some of the mine fields that the North Koreans built to deter Koreans from either going North or South. Next we visited three of the underground tunnels that the North Koreans had constructed to gain access to South Korea. One of the tunnels was three miles long. All three caves were discovered before the North Koreans could utilize them. Finally we went to a small camp at the DMZ. The U. S. Army had control of the camp. Our bus stopped at the gate and a Korean Soldier from the U. S. Army boarded as our tour guide. He cautioned us about the Headquarters Building where we were going because the North Korean Headquarters Building was less than a hundred yards away and their guards kept a watchful eye on all of the tourists that came into the area. We saw the North Korean guards standing their posts looking straight at us and we even saw guards in the windows with binoculars. The tour guide instructed us not to make any sudden moves or gestures at the North Korean guards because they were armed with loaded weapons.

The tour guide took us to a small building with a large conference table in the center. This was where North and South Koreans would have their conferences at one time. Half of the building was in North Korea and half was in South Korea, including the conference table and chairs. South Korea had guards inside at each door and the guards stood motionless at the attack position for anyone who would try to open the door at the North Korean end of the building. On the outside of the North Korean side of the door was a North Korean armed guard. The South Korean guards didn't move or talk but they let us take photos with them as long as we didn't touch them.

It made us all nervous to know that one false move or gesture by any of the tourists could have caused an international incident that could've possibly led to someone getting either injured or killed. It could've taken the smallest thing to set one of the North Koreans off. North Korea had been under sanctions for many years and their economy had really suffered tremendously. We were told by the tour guide that if you flew over the country of Korea at night, you can tell the difference between North and South. South Korea is lit up by a full-scale electric power company and North Korea is dim and gloomy due to poorly maintained power sources. There was also a shortage of food, gas, medical facilities and many more of the resources it took to stabilize a country and its people. We could see where the animosity and hatred toward South Korea and America came from. Needless to say, we had a great experience at the DMZ and I made it a point to stop at the souvenir store to purchase a shirt stating, "I survived the DMZ between North and South Korea."

"Army Camp at the DMZ (Demilitarized Zone).
North Korean Headquarters in the background."

Military Intelligence

In March of 2008, while still stationed in Okinawa, Japan, a fellow Marine, his wife, and I decided to take a trip to Mainland, Japan, specifically Tokyo and Yokota, Singapore and Malaysia. We had talked about this trip after our trip to Bangkok, Thailand the previous year. The first thing that we had to do was, get our leave approved, then submit an anti-terrorism force protection plan for the duration of our trip. The purpose of the plan was to alert the U. S. Embassy that we'll be in their geographical arena. We sought the advice of our Anti-Terrorism Force Protection Officer who laid out the template for our Thailand trip. Our plan was to catch an AMC (Air Mobility Command) flight from Kadena Air Force Base, Japan to Yokota Air Force Base, Japan, spend a couple of days in Tokyo, catch another AMC flight to Singapore, spend a week there and then fly to Malaysia for a few days. AMC flights were free flights for service members and their families. These were space available flights to military bases all over the world and to a few commercial airports. All of this had to be explained in our plan which is mandatory if you're traveling overseas.

The next thing we had to do was receive an intelligence brief from the Marine Corps Base Security Manager. The brief took place the day prior to our trip and I must say that the gentleman that briefed us made it clear that our well-being was really at risk while taking this trip. He pointed out that although there was very little threat in Mainland, Japan, Singapore and Malaysia posed a very serious threat for U. S. citizens and service members. He mentioned some of the Muslim terrorists groups operating in Asia, specifically the Abu Sayyaf operating in the southern Philippines that the U. S. was helping the Filipino government fight. He also mentioned that a well known leader of one of the groups was captured and escaped from jail about two weeks earlier. It really seemed to us that the Security Manager was trying to intimidate the three of us from taking the trip. After about fifteen minutes of the rhetoric, I informed him that I was Muslim and that I had been to Malaysia three times without incident and at no time did my family or I feel threatened at all. I probably could have given him a lecture on being a military member in Malaysia because of my Muslim background. The Security Manager, being the intelligence expert that he was, probably felt offended. Before we left the brief, he requested that upon my return from the trip, that I come in and back brief him on the Muslim intelligence atmosphere in the two countries. I told him that I would.

We departed to Yokota the next day on a military MD-11. Since we were both Master Gunnery Sergeants (E-9s), we had the luxury of waiting at the terminal in the V.I.P. lounge. The lounge was free of noisy children and was equipped with a television, telephones, computers, free snacks, a very relaxing atmosphere, and we boarded the aircraft first. We arrived in Yokota early afternoon and we made our way to billeting. Shortly after, we were on the train to Tokyo. We arrived in Tokyo and went directly to an Indian restaurant that my family and I had visited during one of our previous trips to Tokyo. Next on our agenda was to visit the military New Sanno Hotel that service members occupy when they come to Tokyo. I wanted to see if one of my Muslim Moroccan brothers was still working in the restaurant on the second floor. Unfortunately, he was in Morocco at the time but I met another brother who was working there from Bangladesh. We walked to a few sights in Tokyo and then we were back on the train to Yokota. The next day we were up early, ready for another day in Tokyo. We caught the daily bus that ran from billeting to the New Sanno in the morning and back at night. That day we walked through downtown Tokyo to the Tokyo Tower, one of the most popular landmarks of the city. After the Tokyo Tower we went back to the hotel to wait for our transportation back to Yokota. Two days later we were on another MD-11 for Singapore.

It felt good to arrive in Singapore after a seven hour flight. We processed through immigration and a gentleman that we met on the flight offered us a ride to the Naval Base where we were billeting. The gentleman was a retired Army Sergeant First Class, originally from Cambodia who was residing in Singapore. It was a twenty-five minute ride to the Navy Base in Sembawang and we caught a glimpse of many sights as we rode through the city. My first impression of Singapore was overwhelming. It had a mixture of three cultures—Chinese, Indian, and Malay—and the streets were unlike any streets I've seen in many countries; they were clean. You couldn't even chew gum on the streets! I recall an incident that occurred in Singapore a few years back when an American was publicly caned for spraying graffiti on cars. I also recall passing by two masjids, one of which was located close to the Naval Base.

Billeting was located in the housing area of large beautiful homes. The billeting quarters were surrounded by barbed-wire fencing and guarded twenty-four hours a day. After check-in, we walked to the U. S. Naval Yard for a bite to eat. Each time we left our quarters, we had to pass through the security guards and while presenting my identification card to the guard, we both recognized each other's names. He asked if I was a Muslim and I told him yes. He was very excited that I was a Muslim and turned around to tell his co-worker who was Muslim also. I was with my friends so I told them that I would come to talk with them later. When we returned to the compound, the guards and I chatted for a while. They seemed fascinated that I was an American visiting their country and even more fascinated that I was a Muslim in the military. We talked at length about a few issues including my Pilgrimage to Hajj, how many Muslims there were in the U. S. military, Singapore's economy and culture, the best places to shop, and the locations of the area masjids. We even talked about the Islamic terrorist that escaped from jail two weeks before we arrived. From what I gathered from our conversations, they both had a great deal of respect for America and especially the American military. They asked questions about which branch of the military was the best, what I did on my off time, what were my favorite foods, and so on.

We conversed about three hours until their shift change, in which two more Muslim brothers took over the security. They too were shocked and excited that I was an American military Muslim. After our introductions, I departed for my room to get some sleep. The next morning while coming through the gate, a new shift was on and it felt as if they already knew me. Apparently the previous guards told them about me. These guards welcomed me with open arms and told me to let them know if there was anything we needed while we were there. We really felt at home there and contrary to what the Security Manager had briefed, we didn't feel threatened at all.

That day we toured the Naval Base and then caught the bus to the train station for transportation into some of the major cities on the island. We purchased transportation cards that enabled us to ride the bus and train until the cash value was depleted. When that happened we just put more money on the cards. We were really amazed about how clean the train stations were, not to mention that there were no trash receptacles on any of them. The Singapore government didn't allow eating or drinking in any of the stations or on the trains. Some of the trains were very crowded and that led me to keep thinking back to the security brief that was given by the Security Manager about the anti-American sentiment in Singapore. We still did not feel threatened in any way.

My friends were interested in visiting the world famous Raffels Hotel where the Singapore Sling drink originated back in 1921. I was more content just visiting the different masjids and getting photos of them. We arrived at the hotel and they went in to try the drink, I waited out on the patio reviewing my photos. Muslims were not allowed to go into bars. Alcohol was considered the handy-work of Satan and it had destroyed many lives. They returned in about thirty minutes and I asked how the drinks were. They told me that they paid about $28 for each drink and that they were like any other Singapore Sling. Although the drinks set them back about $56, they were able to say that they had tasted the original Singapore Sling.

After leaving Raffels we were back on the train about three stops to visit two of the most famous masjids in Singapore, the Hajja-Al Fatima, which was the oldest, and the Sultan, which was the largest. Once we departed the train and came up to street level, I began asking for directions. The Sultan Masjid was only a ten minute walk and I was amazed when it came into view. I could see its gold domes two blocks away as the sun glistened off of them. It was located on the corner of a large intersection and I took photos from three or four angles. My next task was to find the Hajja-Al Fatima Masjid which was about another ten minutes walk. This masjid was located in a grassy park. As I took photos, the adhan (call to prayer) started and one of the brothers motioned for me to come in to pray with them. After prayer, we were on the train heading back to the Naval Base.

When we returned to the base, I asked the guards where the closest masjid was so that I could attend morning prayers the next day. There was one located about a mile from where we were billeting. The next morning I was up at 4:45 a.m. to make the 5:15 a.m. prayer time at the masjid. It was pitch dark when I started my walk through the housing area and out to the main road. I passed by groups of shift workers who were getting off from their shift at the shipyard. The thought of the security brief crossed my mind so I tried to walk in the well lit areas for safety. The few vehicles that passed by, provided light also and at that time of morning with the darkness, it would have been very easy for a kidnapping or an attack. The passers-by could clearly see that I was American. I wore my kufee so that they could also see that I was Muslim.

When I reached the masjid, there were about twenty brothers scattered throughout reading Quran and meditating. I went to the far side from the entrance and picked up a Quran. I could see the eyes following me as I walked by. They knew that I was not from the area and were curious to know where I was from. One brother came over to talk to me and shook my hand. He told me his name and asked where I was from. I told him that I was from Japan and that I was in Singapore on vacation. I didn't tell him that I was in the military but I did tell him that I was American. He was glad to hear that I was an American and better yet that I was an American Muslim. We talked until prayer time and afterwards I departed back to billeting. Another brother saw me walking and offered me a ride. I declined for safety reasons but I was overwhelmed by the hospitality that I received.

In the next couple of days, we visited Sentosa Island (a popular tourist attraction similar to an amusement park) two malls and the Singapore Zoo. The zoo was the highlight of Singapore. Although it was raining when we arrived, it did not take away from the excitement of what we experienced. Most memorable were the polar bears, the white Bengal tigers, the orangutans, and the komodo dragons. I had heard and seen so much about komodo dragons on the Animal Planet channel and now I had the opportunity to see one up close and personal. The highlight of the entire zoo experience was the photos that I took with the orangutans. The trainers allowed me to stand in front of them but they warned me that they were extremely strong if they hit or grabbed me. I was able to get the photos without incident.

That night we returned to the zoo for the second part of the experience, the Night Safari, where we're able to ride a tram through the park witnessing the animals in their natural habitat at night. The tram rode through areas where the animals actually walked up to the tram. For the next couple of days we couldn't stop talking about the zoo. The Singapore Zoo definitely rated among the top three zoos that I have visited. I looked forward to returning to Japan to show the family the photos.

The next day we made plans to visit Malaysia, the bordering country. I had been to Malaysia several times and I told my friends that they would probably enjoy it. Malaysian culture is the same as Singapore, comprised of Malays, Chinese, and Indians. Singapore used to be a part of Malaysia until it was given its independence. The only difference was that Malaysia was ninety-five percent Muslims versus the forty-five percent in Singapore.

We were able to book flights into the capital, Kuala Lumpur, for a reasonable price. We booked a hotel next to the Kuala Lumpur Tower which is one of the main attractions of the city. We landed at the K. L. Airport, passed through immigration and waited outside for a taxi. Our taxi driver was Indian and very excited about meeting us. He informed us that he was not only a taxi driver but a tour guide as well. We set up a tour for the following day.

Once we were checked into our hotel, we ventured out to tour the city. First stop was the world famous Petronas Towers which were featured in the movie 'Enchantment'. At one time the towers were the tallest structures in the world. Although I had seen the towers several times before, we were in awe with the two majestic structures. We went directly to the base of the structures and as we looked up, we were unable to see the top floors without hurting our necks. The only way to view the entire structures from the base was to lie down and look up. This was how I took a few of my photos. On our way to the towers, we ran into an old friend that used to drive for the U. S. Embassy when I visited previously. He was given instructions by the Marine Detachment Commander, a good friend of mine, to take us anywhere we wanted to go while visiting. What a coincidence to run into him again after seven years. We returned later that evening for night shots that were even more spectacular.

That night we wanted Arab cuisine so we went out in search of an Arab restaurant. It wasn't long before we found one shaped like a Bedouin tent. From half of a block away we could smell the aroma of the oven baked bread and kabaabs. We ate our fill and headed back to the hotel. At 11:00 p.m. the streets were still bustling with people shopping and enjoying Kuala Lumpur's night life. I was surprised to see that more Arabs had migrated to Malaysia. In my previous three visits, Arab presence was very scarce. Many now had their own businesses. I've heard that many Saudis relocated to Malaysia because the Islamic laws are more lenient in Malaysia. We made it back to the hotel and retired for the evening.

The next day we had our taxi driver pick us up for a tour. We toured various places that included the ancient Hindu caves, a Buddhist Shrine, the Malaysian War Memorial, a pewter and jewelry factory, and the Putrajaya, the Blue, and the National Masjids. It was great having a tour guide, not only did we get the opportunity to see certain sights, but we had the origin and history explained also. I've learned from past experiences that it's always good to be accompanied by a native when you're touring a foreign country. It helped to neutralize the language barrier and it keeps the nationals from taking advantage of you when you're shopping.

On our last day in K. L., I went out early that morning in search for masjids. I could see a few from my hotel window and I figured that if I walked in their direction I would find them. I located about five and took some wonderful photos for my collection. Once I returned to the hotel, we set off to Little India where we heard that the shopping was good. As we entered Little India, we noticed the Little India Masjid. Of course I got a photo before we started shopping. I ran in and out of many Islamic stores searching for prayer rugs and scarves for a friend. Shopping in Little India was very rewarding. The prices were the best that we had seen in K. L. I was able to completely fill my luggage.

After lunch the following day, we were back at the airport for our flight back to Singapore. We received a ride back to the terminal with the same gentleman who delivered us to the Naval Base. He was remaining in Singapore with his family and did us a huge favor by assisting us. Our flight back to Yokota was great as I reminisced about what we did and the places we visited in Singapore and Malaysia. What an experience! I couldn't wait to return before I retired in three years.

Our day back in Yokota was utilized solely for relaxing. Originally we were going to wait for the AMC flight back to Kadena but we heard that the flight had been moved to another day. We decided to book a commercial flight back to Okinawa. This eliminated the waiting as we were anxious to get back to tell our friends and family what we had experienced. Although I said that I would, I didn't back-brief the Security Manager about the safety conditions of Malaysia or Singapore. The information that he briefed was so far from what we experienced and I didn't want to embarrass him. This only led me to believe that his sources and their sources-which were our Higher Headquarters-were providing inaccurate intelligence concerning Muslims in the Far East. This didn't surprise me in the least.

"The Sultan Masjid is largest Masjid in Singapore."

Putrajaya Masjid in Putrajaya, Malaysia

"Two of the most popular attractions at the Singapore Zoo, the Orangutans and the Komodo Dragons."

Tokyo Graduation 2008

In October of 2007, I was notified by the University of Maryland administration that I had enough credits to graduate from the university with my Bachelor's Degree in Sociology. They also informed me in writing that I had the options of graduating in Okinawa, Korea, or in Mainland, Japan in Tokyo. Without a doubt or hesitation I chose Tokyo because that gave the family another opportunity to visit the wonderful city and to enjoy what it had to offer again. We visited Tokyo a few times but there were still sights to see and things to do there that we hadn't done during our previous trips, like visit Tokyo Disney and staying at the Hardy Barracks. I sent in my graduation funds and cap and gown fee, while my wife made commercial flight reservations through a local travel agency. I also purchased invitations to send to the family but I knew that none of them would be able to make it. It made me feel good to send them because it was part of the graduation process.

On our previous trips to Tokyo we flew military space available "Space A" out of Kadena Air Force Base to Yokota Air Force Base on the Mainland and we caught the train to Tokyo. On this occasion, time was of the essence so we couldn't afford to fly space available and take the chance of missing my graduation. I waited a long time for that opportunity and I had sacrificed many days and nights writing papers and studying to finish up my curriculum. I promised my parents back in 1981 when I enlisted that I would get my degree. It had been many years since then, but after being stationed with units that deployed for operational commitments on a regular basis, procrastination, and a switch of majors, my dream had come into fruition. I finally had my opportunity to walk across that stage and receive my diploma.. Graduation date was set for 7 April 2008.

In addition to visiting some of the sights in Tokyo, I had another opportunity to see two Muslim brothers that I met back in 2001 on a previous trip. One was from Bangladesh and the other was from Morocco. They both worked in the snack bar on the second floor of the New Sanno Hotel. The New Sanno was a military 4-Star hotel where most military families stayed when they went to Tokyo. I met them one day when I stopped through to get a snack. Once they told me where they were from, I knew that they were Muslims. I told them that I was Muslim also and they seemed really surprised. I told the Moroccan brother that we had gone to Morocco and that really added fire to the conversation. My family and I had visited the city of Casablanca where he was from. I was the first military Muslim that they had met at the hotel. I looked forward to seeing them both again.

We departed Okinawa two days prior to graduation. This was our first time flying into Haneda Airport and catching the train to the Hardy Barracks. We looked forward to the experience. It was a two hour flight to Haneda. Our next task was to find the train that was headed to Roppongi, the district where our hotel was located. The graduation was to be held at the New Sanno Hotel which was walking distance from our hotel. We reserved rooms at Hardy Barracks, a remodeled Army Barracks that was more economical than the New Sanno. It didn't have the same amenities as the Sanno, but the rooms were nice, they served continental breakfast, they had movies, and they had an exchange. I stayed there a few years back when I visited Tokyo.

We found the train that led us out of Haneda Airport. We purchased our tickets through the machines that lined the walls there. Of course we had to use Japanese currency and it was a good thing that we had exchanged currency before leaving Okinawa. We had to transfer at a larger station about twenty minutes away. There, we were lost but a kind Japanese man took us to the train that we had to take. At that time of the day, the trains were pretty crowded and our luggage didn't help the situation any. We've traveled on many Japanese trains and it was always the same scenario. The working class Japanese would board the train and would sleep in-between stops, especially in the evenings. Somehow they always seemed to wake up at the right time they were supposed to get off.

We learned years ago that when the trains are crowded and the doors opened, you had to move quickly or you were pushed out of the way. It seems like it was part of the culture, and they didn't excuse themselves. We traveled another hour on the train watching the sights and keeping an eye on the stations as we rolled by. We reached Roppongi Station and that was our time to depart the train. We walked out of the train station to a line of taxi cabs and we told the drivers "Hardy Barracks." Immediately, they knew where to go. We checked into our rooms and then darted into the streets of Tokyo.

Our first stop was an Indian restaurant about six blocks down. We left there full and then walked another ten minutes to the New Sanno

Hotel where the graduation would be held. The lobby was already filled with graduation candidates and their families and we still had two days until graduation. We checked out the schedule of events for graduation day. We had to arrive three hours before graduation for rehearsal, caps and gowns, and photos.

I then walked to the second floor restaurant to see if my two Muslim brothers were still working there. I didn't see the Moroccan brother when I walked in so I asked if he was working that day. Unfortunately, he had taken his family to Morocco for vacation, so I missed him this trip. The brother from Bangladesh was not working that day either so I missed him also. I did manage to meet another brother from Sri Lanka that was employed at the restaurant. We talked for a while and then he asked if I had done my evening prayer. I hadn't, so he took me to the room where the workers sleep to pray the Maghrib Prayer. After the prayer I reunited with the family and we visited the Tours Office to make plans to visit the Tokyo Tower the next day. We grabbed another train schedule and map and walked back to the hotel. The kids rented movies on the way in and that's how we ended the day.

The next morning we were up for continental breakfast and then to the train station heading for the Tokyo Tower. We took the train as close as we could get and we walked about fifteen minutes to the base of the tower. Although it didn't open for another half hour, a line had already started forming. When they opened we purchased our tickets and took the elevator to the top. We had such a magnificent view of Tokyo from there. We could see for miles. We made sure that we rotated to every angle so that we didn't miss anything. We tried to find Tokyo Disney but it was too far off. We stayed at the tower for about an hour.

We spent the rest of the day touring Tokyo until we needed a break. We went back to the rooms to rest and to decide where we would eat dinner that evening. We decided to walk around in Roppongi that evening to find a place to eat. We spotted Tony Romas and Fridays, and Fridays was our choice. Afterwards, we stopped at Cold Stone for dessert on our way back to the room. Night life in Tokyo was overwhelming. The streets are lined with clubs and bars and people were elbow to elbow while walking on the sidewalks. There was a lot of hustling, human trafficking and prostitution happening on the streets of Tokyo so we didn't stay out there that long. The walk to and from dinner was the extent of our night life in Tokyo.

Graduation day couldn't come fast enough. We were at the Sanno at 10:00 a.m. for rehearsal, cap and gown issue and photos. The University of Maryland had everything and everyone organized. They had specific rooms for those receiving their Associate's, Bachelor's, and Master's degrees. We lined up in order so that the Mistress of Ceremony could practice on the difficult names to pronounce. After rehearsal we were instructed to be in place forty-five minutes prior to the ceremony starting. The ceremony started as scheduled with the graduates marching in first, followed by the University President, the faculty, and the guest speaker. They announced the candidates for their Master's degrees first, then Bachelor's followed by the candidates for their Associate's.

When our row stood to march up to the stage, the promise that I made to my parents was embedded in my thoughts. I was finally graduating and it really felt good. The only issue I had to worry about now was the Mistress of Ceremony pronouncing my name incorrectly and not tripping on the stairs as I approached the stage to receive my diploma. The evolution went very well. I even heard my family applauding when my name was called. At the conclusion of the ceremony, we were instructed to change our tassels to the other side of our caps. We were then graduates of the University of Maryland and another mission was accomplished.

After the ceremony we socialized and then had an elaborate reception. The University had an array of Japanese dishes and desserts to consume. From sushi, to teriyaki chicken, to prime rib steak, it was all there for our choosing. Despite the fact that we were enjoying the cuisine and fellowship, it was getting late so we caught taxis back to our rooms.

The following day we took the family to Tokyo Disney for the entire day. We had already experienced Disney World in Orlando, Florida and Disney Land in California of which both were better than Tokyo Disney. One thing that we noticed about Tokyo Disney that we hadn't noticed at the other two parks was the fact that they had an Arab section that displayed some Arab culture, including foods. We definitely got a kick out of that.

The next morning we were back on a flight to Okinawa. While I was relaxing on the flight, I reflected back to when I left Virginia State University to enlist in the military with the foresight of the military helping me to pursue my degree. The military had done just that. While on active duty, I had to stretch it out class by class but the overall result came out the same. I was forever grateful to all of my supervisors that supported me during my years of pursuing my degree. I also gave a special thanks to my guidance counselors that provided direction, my family that allowed me to utilize countless hours studying and attending classes when we could have been doing family things, and Almighty God for the patience, the drive and determination to fulfill one of my lifelong dreams.

"Graduation at the New Sanno Hotel, Tokyo, Japan, April 2008."

"Under the Petronas Towers in Kuala Lumpur, Malaysia."

Chapter Seven

SEMPER FIDELIS

I departed San Antonio on June 20, 2008 at 4:00 a.m., en route to my final duty station. I figured that I would get a jump on the morning traffic if I left early. It took me nine hours to reach El Paso, close to the New Mexico border. The route I took through Texas, New Mexico, and Arizona was mostly desert and cactus with a small town sprouting up every now and then. The trip was painstakingly boring and my oldie but goodie compact disk collection followed suit. I tried the radio off and on but they mostly aired Spanish stations that spoke too fast for me to understand. It was a relief to stop to fill up with gas and to stretch out my back and legs. Around 7:30 p.m. the sun was starting to set so I decided to stop at a hotel in Phoenix, Arizona, catch up on my prayers, get some rest and start traveling early the next morning. The next morning, directly after the Fajr prayer (early morning prayer), I started the last leg of my trip to San Diego. From Phoenix, I roughly had about a six hour drive and it would be a breeze to drive the six hours compared to the fifteen I drove the previous day.

While driving my three state trek to California from San Antonio, I thought about how my colleagues at the new office would accept me as being a Muslim. I had heard of and had witnessed so many cases where relationships had been cordial until Muslims mentioned the fact that they are Muslim, both military and non-military. My predecessor had my personal information for six months, so my colleagues should have already known what my religious preference was. I always mentioned to my Muslim brothers and sisters that we as Muslims are protected in the military. Most commanders did not tolerate any form of discrimination in their ranks and they had Equal Opportunity Advisors and Representatives that were designated in their commands to ensure that members were not facing discrimination whether racial, ethnic, religious, or sexual. Did discrimination still exist? Of course it did. I've learned that most religious discrimination cases were by service members who had deployed to Iraq or Afghanistan and had left those countries with a bitter attitude toward the locals. A year or two after the start of Operation Iraq Freedom, it was mandated that mandatory training be conducted for all those deploying in support of the war on terrorism. Still, we had service members that showed a wanton disregard for Islamic culture and traditions that were reflected by Muslims in the military. I served with military members from Iraq, Somalia, Palestine, and even Iran. Members from each of these countries had faced discrimination in all of the branches of service. This was my personal opinion but I can't see discrimination prevalent in one branch and not in the others.

I also thought about reuniting with the four military Muslims that I served with in Okinawa, Japan, all of which chose San Diego as their domicile. There was one Navy couple that was released from active duty in 2007, one Navy Dental Technician who was released in 2000, and a Marine released in 2005. I looked forward to sitting down with them and seeing what had transpired in their lives since the last time we saw each other.

I approached San Diego around mid-day after being held up at a routine car inspection near the Mexican border. The California Highway Patrol and Immigration routinely checked for illegal aliens that made it across the border and headed north into the more populated areas of San Diego. Immigration did not give me a detailed inspection. I guess that they recognized by the sticker on my windshield that I was in the military. They asked if I had anyone in the car with me and they could clearly see that I didn't. They waved me through.

As I continued north through the California hills, I saw structures of cities off in the distance. This was a far cry from what I had grown accustomed to seeing while traveling through the desolate New Mexico and Arizona deserts where all that I saw were sand dunes and cactus. As I drove up and down the hills, I anxiously awaited the next mile sign that showed I was getting closer to the city of San Diego.

I reached the city around 2:00 p.m. and I was pretty excited about seeing the Marine Corps Recruit Depot. During my 27 years of service, I had never been stationed on the west coast. I followed my map and lost my way once I got to the city. I ended up downtown by the harbor. It was really beautiful downtown, and I saw the commercial airlines approaching for landing so I knew that the airport was close. Downtown was in full affect. Corporate executives, hotel workers, city maintenance workers, meter maids, and tourists were amidst the scenery as I looked in all directions. I drove around downtown hoping to see a sign that would put me in the direction of the Depot but no such luck. I stopped and put the Depot address into my GPS and that solved my problem.

I arrived at the Depot in five minutes. It was located that close to downtown. This was home for my last three years in the Corps. Here is where I would accumulate 30 years of active service to our Corps. Here is where I would bid my final farewell to a career that had provided for my family and had allowed us to take advantage of the many opportunities that the military had to offer. Here is where I planned to conduct my retirement ceremony that would conclude the final episode of my career that started back in 1981.

My first weekend in San Diego, I met with the former Dental Technician and his brother who had come from his native country Morocco to study electrical engineering at San Diego State University (SDSU). They invited me to dinner at a local pizza parlor close to his place in Ranchos Penasquitos. He now worked for a local corporation managing data bases and servers. He had gotten married a couple of years ago and now had a beautiful one year old daughter. His wife is Moroccan as well and spoke four languages vice the three that he spoke. I always found it fascinating how most foreigners from the African continent could speak three or four languages and we as Americans struggled at just English. We talked about our families and future plans. We also agreed that I would take my family back to Morocco to visit his family as we did back in 2000. It really felt good to catch up on our life's experiences and I couldn't wait to meet his wife and daughter.

I also visited the former Navy couple that chose to end their military careers in 2007, a year after departing from Okinawa. They also had a beautiful daughter now and were loving life out of the military. With Naval Corpsmen backgrounds, they both worked at a local hospital and his wife stopped working after having the baby. They lived in La Mesa, which was about a twenty-five minute drive from the base here. We sat down over hot tea and we both asked about certain families that we had come in contact with while we were stationed together in Japan back in 2005-2007. I left their home late that Sunday night and they asked me to come back during the week to finish our conversation.

I was unable to see the Muslim Marine that was now discharged from active duty that weekend but I made it a priority to see him the following weekend. He invited me to dinner at his place in La Jolla. The next Saturday I had dinner with him and his wonderful family. He too had gotten married to a native Moroccan and they had a nine month old daughter. He worked for a local limousine service that was well known in the area.

All three of my Muslim families were well established here in San Diego and I was ecstatic about being here with them while I completed my thirty years of service and then retire.

I checked into my unit on the 21st of June and immediately began my check-in process. I met my predecessor and both bosses, along with my office colleague. It took about a week to check in. My first weekend in San Diego, I went in search of the area masjids. There were thirteen located in the San Diego area. I found two within a ten mile radius from the base, the Masjid Abu Bakr, also the Masjid Al Taqwa. The following Friday I attended service at Masjid Abu Bakr. I didn't think that it would be a problem with my boss to attend and it wasn't. The Muslim holy day was Friday and I had seen many service members experience conflict when they asked to attend Friday service. Many leaders felt that you're trying to avoid work. My boss was somewhat familiar with Islamic culture due to a tour in Iraq and the fact that she served as an Equal Opportunity Advisor at one of her previous duty stations.

Our command was contemplating a presentation on Islam for those deploying to operating forces in Iraq and Afghanistan and she asked if I could assist them in doing so. I told her that I already had a couple of power point presentations that I had presented to a couple of commands in Okinawa. She talked with our Battalion Executive Officer and apparently he or the Commanding Officer didn't feel that I was competent or knowledgeable enough on the subject matter to conduct the training for the command. This was after I had spent nine years as the Islamic Lay Leader for all of the branches of service on Okinawa. My boss was told that the command had a Marine Intelligence Officer coming to conduct the training. I had to laugh because I have seen first hand how effective military intelligence was when it came to Islam and Muslims. I've sat in classified briefs and could only shake my head at some of the information that had been gathered for these briefs.

I can recall a U.S. intelligence blunder back in 2004 when U.S. forces bombed a pharmaceutical warehouse in Sudan where intelligence led them to believe that a suspected terrorist was inside. This incident caused a big uproar in the Muslim world. Even after it was determined that the U.S. had made a mistake, our government neither apologized nor compensated the Sudanese for the loss and if they did, it wasn't mentioned in the media. This was just one of many U.S. intelligence oversights. Needless to say, I had very little confidence in U.S. intelligence when it pertained to Islam and Muslims.

Attending the Islamic Center of San Diego or Masjid Abu Bakr could be compared to riding a caravan through the Middle East. Ninety-five percent of the Muslims that attended are of Arab descent. There was a small population of Afghanis and an even smaller population of Americans that worshipped there. Out of the eighteen Arab countries, most of them were represented in the demographics of the masjid. Indians and Pakistanis were strong in numbers and even Iranians worshipped at Abu Bakr which was rare because most Iranians practice a different ideology of Islam called Shi'ism that had drawn much criticism from the rest of the Muslim world. Ninety—percent of the Muslim world was known as Sunni Muslims. Shi'ites as they were called had added rituals to the religion that were considered by Islamic scholars to be out of the realm of Islam, meaning that by doing these practices, you could be considered a non-Muslim. One of their practices is to beat yourself with chains until you bled, to enact the murder of Hassan and Hussain, the grandsons of the Prophet Muhammad (Pbuh). There was nothing in the Islamic doctrine that said to do this and it was considered as bid'ah, an innovation that could have dire consequences in the hereafter. I had known brothers and sisters from

Iran for a long time and I'm still in contact with them. I don't consider them any less of a Muslim than I am.

As I walked through the masjid I heard Arab conversations, along with Urdu spoken by the Pakistanis and Indians, and even Pashtu spoken by the Afghanis. I noticed that most of the foreign Muslims spoke English but when they were in groups they spoke their native tongue. I kept telling myself that I had learn Arabic so that I could converse with them. Arabic was also the language of the Quran, our holy book, and it would've been nice to read and understand the Arabic text. I learned to read Arabic a few years ago with the help of some of the brothers in the community.

It was good to see that the masjid opened for the early morning Fajr prayer and stayed open until after the evening Isha prayer. They had an Islamic school for boys as well as girls and they taught an Islamic curriculum that included Arabic. A store was inside the masjid that opened after every prayer except for the early morning prayer. The store contained items that ranged from foods to Islamic books, and it maintained a steady flow of traffic. Weekends were filled with children's activities at the masjid as well as adult study groups and committee meetings.

The masjid also served the community well. They conducted charitable events and fund raisers that helped families in the community and social organizations like the Council for American Islamic Relations (CAIR). Throughout the United States, CAIR consistently came to the aid of Muslims who had been discriminated against. Just recently after I arrived here in San Diego, we had a situation where a Muslim sister was asked to leave a banking institution because she wore a hijab, or religious head scarf. Management said it was for security reasons. This was the same institution that I utilized. She resorted to exposing the credit union to the local news station that was captured by our local chapter of CAIR. CAIR intervened and the institution apologized and vowed to rewrite their dress policy that will allow religious tolerance like the head scarf. Alhamdulilah (All Praise is to God) for CAIR. May Allah (swt) be pleased with the work that they did for all humanity.

When I attended the masjid I never wore my military uniform. There were Muslims that disliked U.S. military members, primarily because of the Iraq invasion and U.S. foreign policy. More specifically because of the horrendous acts that took place at the Army Abu Ghraib Prison in Bagdad a few years back. Due to the nature of some of those acts, the U.S. military will never be able to make up for what took place there. Although it was the Army that committed the atrocities, some Muslims look at the entire force as being responsible. Many of them were not aware that there were different branches of service in the U.S. Although I did not wear my uniform to the masjid, I had seen a Naval Officer attend in his. In retrospect, I would have loved to talk with him to see how the climate was once he entered. Friday service (Jummah) was so convenient at my two previous duty stations because it was held on the bases. Most of the Muslims wore their uniforms and returned to work right after service.

There was a Pakistani restaurant that I frequented once a week there in Claremont Mesa called Bismillah. The cuisine there was delicious and the majority of its patrons are Muslims. At times the owner would come over to chat with me. I was a regular customer and I wore my kufee at times, so he knew that I was a Muslim. A kufee is a garment that male Muslims wore on their heads, similar to the Jewish yarmulke. Recently I invited some of my military friends to lunch and we came to Bismillah in uniform. Once seated, the owner came over to the table and stated, "I didn't know that you were in the military." He was really flattered to see our military representation support his establishment. He made it a point to come over and check on us every five minutes or so to see if there was anything else we needed. Now when I visited the restaurant, it seemed like I got special attention whether in or out of uniform. I think that had a lot to do with the fact that I was a Muslim who wore the uniform of a service member.

Arabic 101

In September of 2008, I enrolled in my first academic Arabic class. I have attended classes previously taught by brothers in the community. It was now a chance for me to see if what I had learned was beneficial. It was my desire to become more fluent in Arabic so that I was able to converse with my extended Arab family. My class at City College here in San Diego was held on Tuesdays and Thursdays from 4:30 p.m. to 7:30 p.m. and I had no problem getting off from work early to attend. It only took me about ten minutes to get to class here at the downtown campus. Our class was filled to capacity with a mixture of Whites, African Americans, Hispanics and Somalis. A few who attended the class had intentions of working in the Middle East. The majority of the class were Muslims that wanted to learn Arabic as a duty to the religion. We had a few third generation

Arabs in attendance that couldn't speak Arabic and we had a brother in the class from Yemen that spoke fluent Arabic. He basically took the class to maintain his grade point average. This class was taught by a Palestinian sister that had been in the United States for about ten years. She had a Master's Degree in Sociology and her husband a Master's in Business Administration. Her class was great because not only did we learn the language but we learned Arab culture as well.

During the course of the class we had to conduct a ten page presentation on any Arab country of our choice. Also during the course of the class we took a field trip to an Arab restaurant to taste the Arab cuisine and to utilize our language skills. The restaurant we visited was Iraqi and much of their Arab dialect was colloquial. We learned modern standard Arabic. That way we would be able to speak with anyone in most of the Arab speaking countries and they would be able to understand us. The City College Arab Students Association had planned a thirty-day trip to Egypt that would have been ideal but like me, most of the students couldn't afford it. The experience would've been well worth the money but I couldn't afford to lose thirty days leave prior to my retirement.

On days when I left the office late to get to class, I wore my uniform. For some reason, many of my classmates were shocked to see that I was a Marine, and even more shocked to learn that I was a Muslim Marine. This attracted many conversations from the Muslims and non-Muslims. We had five Navy Sailors in our class and they asked the typical Marine questions. The rest of the class asked Marine and Muslim questions basically concerning family, stereotypes, and experiences we had been through.

I'm often asked how I manage to pray five times a day with my work schedule. It's actually pretty easy. Our early morning prayer (Fajr) is before sunrise so that's not an issue. Our early afternoon prayer (Zhour) was around lunch time so that's not a problem either. The late afternoon prayer (Asr) occured during work hours but I delayed it until I returned from work. There were times in the past when I had my own office and I would actually pray there. The evening prayer (Maghrib) and the night prayer (Isha) were conducted after work hours. My classmates often saw me go to an empty classroom during our fifteen minute breaks to pray. My Muslim sisters prayed in the hallway, even with the student traffic. We entered the month of Ramadan while taking the Arabic class and our professor let us break at sunset to break our fast and to do our prayer. This was allowed by the school to accommodate the Muslims.

Although our professor was Muslim, she made it a point not to talk about the religion, but more of the language and culture. There were times that she was asked religious questions and she answered them but most of the time she avoided religious discussions. She was asked why Muslim women have to cover their hair. She answered by saying that it was written in the Quran to do so, but she didn't cover hers. Some Muslim women only cover their hair when they pray.

Overall, the class was very good. It gave me a better understanding and appreciation of the language and Arab culture. I planned to take the second part later the next year after reviewing what I had learned already. There were only two Arabic professors at City College so there was a good chance that I would get the same one.

Islamic Services on the Depot

In October of 2008, I woke up one Sunday morning for the Fajr prayer and decided to stay up afterwards to do laundry. After an hour or two I noticed recruits walking to attend services at the Depot Chapel. I wondered if the Depot was providing Islamic services for the recruits. The following day I went to the Depot Chaplain's office to inquire. I was told by the secretary that they did offer Islamic services and that there was an Imam from one of the local masjids that came every Sunday to conduct the services. I couldn't wait to meet him the following Sunday.

The following Sunday I made my way over to the Recruit Training Regiment (RTR) Chapel to meet him and those who attended service. The chapel had a room set aside for each faith group and they all were supported by the Depot Chaplain. In the military, service members are allowed to practice any faith they desire as long as it is not detrimental to themselves or those affiliated with them. I walked in and greeted everyone but I didn't want to disrupt the service. There were about twelve to fifteen recruits attending. Some were curious about Islam, some were Muslims, and the others just wanted to get away from their drill instructors for a while. For the most part, they were all pretty attentive. I talked with a few of them after service as well as the Imam. The brother made a forty-five minute drive down every Sunday and had been doing this for the past twenty-one years. This was strictly voluntary and there were not too many people that would sacrifice their Sunday family time to do this. I told him if he ever wanted to take a break that I would sit in for him to conduct the services. Besides his volunteer work here on the Depot, he was the Assistant Imam at Masjid Al-Taqwa here downtown. May Allah be pleased with him for spreading the true meaning of Islam.

The United Servicemen's Organization (USO)

For twenty-eight years, my family and I had utilized the services that the United Servicemen's Organization (USO) had to offer. I recall my days in Okinawa as a Private First Class when most of my time away from the office was spent there. The USO provided long distance phone service, food, games, and tours that made our six month deployment a lot more pleasant. I suffered from homesickness, as did many others because that was my first deployment away from family. My first daughter was born one month before we deployed. It was safe to say that the USO was my outlet for the duration of the deployment. The USO was where I could go whenever I had a bad day and it was my home away from home.

I also remember the USO at the Seattle Airport where my family and I stayed overnight waiting for our flight to the east coast. My father had passed, and we were on our way to Virginia on emergency leave. Traveling from Okinawa, we were already tired and hungry, so the USO saved us from getting a hotel and going out to find dinner. We were accommodated with beds, food, internet, and games for the children until our flight the next day. We never had to leave the airport.

The USO had been a home to service members world-wide and its staff and volunteers made you extremely proud to have served our country. When I arrived in San Diego without my family, I knew that I would have a lot of spare time on my hands. I decided to utilize some of my spare time volunteering at the downtown USO. As Muslims, we are responsible for giving charity and doing charitable deeds. Volunteering definitely fell into that category. I was just trying to give a little back to the organization that had always been there for my family and me. I visited the Airport USO to talk with the Director but he wasn't in. He's was a retired Sergeant Major from the Depot here. I then went to the Downtown USO for a chat with their Director. She told me that they could use volunteers on Tuesday evenings to serve food and to clean up after dinner. Every Tuesday they had organizations that sponsored dinner for the military and their families. All of the organizations and USO volunteers did a wonderful job of preparing, serving and providing our military families of day free of cooking and the opportunity to enjoy each other's camaraderie. They also gave away door prizes during dinner for children and the adults. It was a pleasure to see the children's faces light up when they won. I had a great feeling of satisfaction when I left the USO every Tuesday night. At that time, I couldn't think of anything better that I could be doing.

The Wounded Warrior Project

The Marine Corps had a way of taking care of their own and one of those ways was through the Wounded Warrior Project. The project was designed to provide medical treatment, counseling, mentorship, and tangible support to those Marines and Sailors that had been casualties at war. Contrary to popular belief, not only did they provide these services to wounded Marines and Sailors, but to the mentally challenged as well.

In February of 2009, I visited the Wounded Warrior Project at Balboa Hospital here in San Diego. I wanted to know if I would be able to do any volunteering there for the warriors. I met with the Commanding Officer and First Sergeant who briefed me about the project. They took me on a tour through their complex and I even had the opportunity to meet a few of the warriors. They explained that regardless of their injuries, they tried to keep them active. Although injured, most still carried out an array of daily duties not affiliated with their military occupational specialties. The warriors had a pretty nice set-up at the complex. They had spacious suites as living quarters, a gym, a lounge, recreation room and a snack bar. The project received donations and gifts from corporations and families across the United States. Many of the warriors had received laptop computers, free tickets to NFL and Major League Baseball games, and if their families would like to visit San Diego, their hotel expenses were paid for. The entire project was centered and focused on honoring and empowering these warriors. Their goal was to ensure that after their injuries, they're able to go out in society to find jobs and utilize the skills learned here to their full potential. The project was fully staffed and didn't need any volunteers there at the complex. I would be able to volunteer at some of the special events they have scheduled in the area.

Special Premier

On February 22, 2009, two of my close Muslim brothers and I attended the premier of the movie "MOZLYM." The movie was filmed here in San Diego and was casted from the local community. We registered on-line in advance to see the movie and the producer anticipated a standing room only crowd. The movie premiered on the campus of University of California at San Diego and the two showings were filled to capacity. Muslims and non-Muslims enjoyed the movie and according to the surveys completed after the movie, it was well worth the five dollar donation. Special recognition was given to the San Diego Film Commission and the local churches and masjids for helping to make the film. The brother of a well known comedian, both of whom are Muslims, was in attendance and offered assistance in promoting the movie nationwide. The producers of the movie used an unorthodox spelling "MOZLYM" to symbolize the misunderstanding of Islam in the west. The proper way to spell the term was "Muslim," and it was pronounced differently also.

The theme of the movie was redirected from gang violence to Muslim violence. Innocent Muslims had gotten a bad rap because many Muslims misrepresented the religion. Islam was a religion of peace, exemplified by a vast majority of Muslims. It was a very small percentage that misrepresented our way of life. The media was largely responsible for incorrect information written and shown about Muslims. I had seen and experienced first hand some of the rhetoric that ignorant non-Muslims expressed about Muslims. Whenever I had the opportunity to educate non-Muslims about Islam, I took advantage of it. One of my goals was to help bridge the gap between Muslims and all of the other faith groups.

Muslims Making Progress

On March 14, 2009, I had the opportunity and privilege of meeting and listening to a Muslim Congressman from Minnesota speak at the Annual Council for American Islamic Relations (CAIR) Dinner. The Congressman held the title of the first Muslim Congressman in the United States. He actually took his oath to office on the Holy Quran that was once owned by Thomas Jefferson. The dinner was held at the Four-Points Sheraton Hotel and it was very difficult to find an empty seat in the ballroom. Although the tickets were a bit pricey, I could not miss the opportunity to attend. CAIR had dedicated professional assistance for many cases where Muslims were being mistreated or discriminated against. CAIR was one of the only organizations that had been in the forefront of justice for Muslims.

That night, the Congressman spoke about Muslims making a positive impact on society. As Muslims, it was an obligation for us to do so. He also spoke about the conflict in Palestine and what we could do to help. He gave us first hand knowledge of what's happening there. He had visited Palestine a month earlier and witnessed the blatant genocide of the Palestinian people. He walked through rubble from schools, hospitals, and homes. He mentioned several times about the physical and mental devastation the Palestinians had experienced as a result of the Israeli air attacks and shelling.

The Congressman alluded to the fact that although there were rockets being fired out of Palestine, the Israelis took advantage of every opportunity they could to shell parts of Palestine regardless of where the rockets were coming from. Excessive bombing was responsible for most of the Palestinian fatalities.

The Congressman's appearance at the dinner paid enormous dividends for CAIR. After he spoke, CAIR was able to generate much needed funds for their cause. The insight that I gained from his lecture was passed on to those who were ignorant about the plight of the Palestinians.

Islamic School of San Diego (ISSD)

On May 2, 2009, I attended a fund raiser for the Islamic School of San Diego. Apparently the school's expenses exceeded its contributions, which put their budget in the red. The school was founded in 1992 and was the only Islamic school in the San Diego County, which consisted of thirteen masjids. The mission of the school was to facilitate the development of an Islamic personality well informed to live in accordance with the precepts of Islam. The staff consisted of 17 teachers, a principal and finance assistant, and a Board of Educators. Of the 147 students, grades kindergarten through eighth were represented at the school and present at the dinner were four alumni that reflected on their success after attending. They each spoke about the balance between Islamic education and the traditional curriculums taught at ISSD. Each of the alumni graduated with college degrees. One was pursuing a Master's and another had been accepted at the Harvard Divinity School with a concentration in Islamic studies. One sister was now a teacher at ISSD.

As we enjoyed dinner, the ISSD staff showed videos of the daily routines of the different grades. The videos viewed into the classrooms and gave us a good picture of history, Arabic, and science classes. The ballroom where we dined was lined with science projects completed by the students. It was evident that the school was paying dividends. Many of the projects were constructed at a level far more advanced than the grades reflected in the write-ups. One in particular that caught my eye was about the five most popular languages spoken around the world. It included statistics, graphs and maps of the continents where the languages were spoken. The intent of the project was to encourage people to learn a second language. The ability to speak a second language opened opportunities for employment, professional development, and cultural diversity.

After dinner we were treated by a lecture from a renowned scholar and lecturer. He lectured about the accomplishments and the contributions that Muslims have made for mankind. Science, mathematics, art and agriculture were some of the subjects that distinguished Muslims as some of the finest innovators that this world has ever known. What many failed to realize was that the cradle of civilization as mentioned in biblical text was once called the Ur of Chaldees, which later became known as Mesopotamia and is now called Iraq. There was a time when Iraq was well known for its libraries of knowledge. Large portions of these libraries were burned during invasions.

The fund raiser was a huge success. It unofficially generated about $65,000 from the Muslim community, and that was not counting disclosed donations. I applaud the fact that the Muslim community was able to do this without any outside help. This was proof that the Muslim community in San Diego was growing and that there were professional, successful Muslims in the area. We pray that this Islamic school was the first of a successful line of Islamic schools across the county.

Exposed at the 2008 Marine Corps Ball

It was traditional in the Marine Corps that we celebrated the birthday of our Corps every year. For 233 years, members of this distinguished gun club, past and present, had done this faithfully, without question. This year while stationed here at my last command before retirement, we celebrated the birth of our illustrious Corps on November 9, 2008 at the Downtown Sheraton Hotel.

Once the date and location were confirmed, I contacted my wife so that she could make flight reservations to come out to attend. Throughout my career she had attended and had thoroughly enjoyed them. During my past two years in Okinawa, my entire family, minus my son who was away attending college, attended and enjoyed themselves also, especially my granddaughter. Immediately my wife booked a flight and began to ramble through her wardrobe for an outfit to wear. She called me the next day and said that she wanted to wear something special that year. Never before had she worn the traditional Islamic head-scarf to the Ball but this year it was her desire. She began searching Islamic clothing websites for something nice.

I also contacted one of my Muslim families to see if they wanted to attend that year. Although they were both Corpsmen and spent eight years in the Navy, neither had ever attended a Marine Corps Ball. My brother cordially accepted my invitation but told me that his wife would probably not make it because of their infant daughter. He asked about the attire and I told him that a suit was feasible. He went out and purchased one shortly thereafter. This was the first suit that he had ever owned and he was excited about attending.

My wife arrived the day prior to the ball and we went through our same ritual as we do every time she visited San Diego. We went to our favorite restaurant, Bismillah, and her favorite coffee spot, Seven-Eleven. She showed me her outfit and I must say that it looked very nice, head-scarf and all. I then thought about how the other Marines and their wives would react when we walked into the ballroom. There were not many people here on the Depot that knew that I'm Muslim and I was sure that it would be the talk of the ball.

Along with the announcement of the ball came a request for volunteers to act as Cake Escorts and Swordsmen for the cake cutting ceremony. Traditionally, there was a Swordsman for each enlisted pay-grade. I volunteered this year just as I had done in the past. The duties of the Swordsmen were not difficult. I just had to brush up on my sword manual and after we rehearsed for three days, everyone looked sharp for the ceremony.

It was also customary that during the cake cutting ceremony, the first piece of cake be given to the oldest, and then youngest Marines. That year, I was the oldest Marine in attendance therefore I would be the recipient of the first piece of cake. The Depot Sergeant Major was a year younger than I was so he dodged the honors that year.

On the evening of the ball, my wife dropped me off early so that we could rehearse two more times before the ceremony. She went back to the hotel to dress. The thought came to my mind a few times about how the crowd would react when they saw that we were Muslims. I wasn't too concerned about it because most of the people that knew me knew what type of a person I was and I thought that this would overshadow the negative stereotypes that some had against Muslims.

My wife returned to the hotel during the cocktail hour and she called while the valet parked the car. I picked her up in the driveway and escorted her inside. Once we entered the corridor, I could see people staring at her and I heard a voice from the right echo, "That outfit looks nice." I assumed that this was the first time that she had seen a Muslim with the head-scarf and formal gown. The combination she chose really looked good as the sparkle in the black head-scarf complimented her black gown. As we walked into the Ballroom, I watched the heads turn and I read the lips of a few say, "I didn't know that MGySgt Camp was a Muslim." We walked to our seats and we were greeted by one of my colleagues and his wife as we sat down. A few minutes later I walked out to the lobby to pick up my brother. I almost did not recognize him in his suit. This was the first time that I had seen him in a suit. Where he was from in the Philippines, he never had use for one.

The escorts and swordsmen had to be in place in the lobby a half hour before the ceremony started. Promptly at 1900 we marched in and took our positions. The escorts wheeled the cake in and took their positions. The guest speaker was escorted in by the Depot Sergeant Major and they took their positions as well. The narrator read the messages of a famous General and the Commandant of the Marine Corps. It was then time for the ceremony where I would taste the first piece of cake and then pass a slice over to the youngest Staff Noncommissioned Officer. When the narrator announced the birthday of the young Staff Sergeant it really made me feel old. I reflected back at the time I was a Staff Sergeant and how old I was when I pinned it on. Times in the Corps have really changed.

After the ceremony and dinner, we watched the pageant of Marines demonstrate the uniforms of Marines past and present and the narrator named the conflicts for each uniform. Displaying the only Navy uniform was the Navy Corpsman who since the existence of the Corps has provided medical attention for Marines on and off the battlefield. The Navy Corpsmen had earned a great deal of respect from our ranks, pasts and present.

We enjoyed the camaraderie at the ball until the music and dancing started. Usually by that time the alcohol started to take affect and things start to get out of hand. It happened every year and it always diminished the significance of the ball. It was a good experience for us, especially for my brother. He'll be able to reflect on it for years to come. I looked forward to answering questions on that Monday but surprisingly the opportunity didn't present itself. Happy 233rd Birthday!

"This photo was taken at the 2008 Marine Corps Recruit Depot, San Diego, Marine Corps Ball."

"This photo was taken during the ceremony at the 2008 Marine Corps Ball, Marine Corps Recruit Depot, San Diego."

"MGySgt Camp was presented with the second piece of cake during the Cake Cutting Ceremony of the 2008 Marine Corps Ball, MCRD, San Diego"

Islamophobia

I was watching Good Morning America News one morning and it featured a story about an attempted robbery that took place in a corner store owned by a Pakistani man. The would-be robber entered the store hooded and hurling a bat at the owner behind the register. He demanded that the owner give him all of the money he had in the register. The owner reached under his counter and pulled out a shotgun. The robber dropped to his knees and asked for mercy. He explained to the owner that he had children that were hungry and needed food.

The owner, out of the kindness of his heart, gave the robber forty dollars out of the register and a loaf of bread. He told the robber to never try to rob anyone again and to get out of the store. Strangely, after the owner's statement, the robber then asked the owner how he could be a Muslim like him. Sounding very sincere, he said that he wanted to be a Muslim like the owner. The owner, realizing the robber's desire, took him through the Shahadah (Declaration of Faith) declaring that there is only one God, and that Muhammad (Pbuh) is the Messenger of God, our seven articles of faith, and adhering to the five pillars of Islam is what makes a non-believer a believer. After administering the Shahadah, the store owner told the robber to wait while he went to the back to get more food for his family. When the owner returned, the robber had fled the store.

The story made national headlines but in some media outlets, the entire story was not revealed. I called home to Texas to see if my wife had heard the story. She replied, "Yes," and began explaining what happened. Her story concluded after the owner gave the robber the forty dollars and the loaf of bread. The critical part of the story was excluded. I asked if that was the rest of the story and she said, "Yes." I told her the rest of the story about the robber asking how he could become Muslim. Why wasn't the rest of the story told, and was this done intentionally? Our Judeo-Christian society does not like to hear about people becoming Muslims. Our society was also content about hearing negative media about Islam. Any story about Islam that portrayed a positive image was not likely to be aired.

I recall the story about the King of Pop, one of the five famous brothers from Gary, Indiana, when he dangled one of his sons over a balcony in England. That story also received national attention for months. The media would not let that story go. Early in 2009, the King of Pop became a Muslim, following suit of his older brother. Here it is the end of June 2009, and this story has not been seen nor heard on television. You can read about the story on Yahoo and Google but it has not been aired via television. Can you imagine the impact that this story would have around the world? The King had been a popular icon throughout his career, and his fans did almost anything to emulate him. Something like this would've started a trend that our society was not ready for. Why didn't the media exploit this story? We knew who controlled the media in the United States, and Israel was still being persecuted for the genocide occurring in Palestine. Anti-Jewish sentiment was at an all-time high at that time and an increase in the Muslim population would only add to that sentiment.

Take the story about our newly elected President. Although he had a Muslim father, he was a Christian. Even after all of the election fall-out about his Christian pastor at his church in Chicago, there were masses of people who still claimed that he was a Muslim. They researched his career and found that he had no ties to any significant Muslim figures or organizations but they still claimed that he was Muslim. We know for a fact that if the President was a Muslim, he would have definitely lost the election. Even though he had great ideas that would help the country, great character, and exemplified outstanding morals and ethics, the fact that he was a Muslim would have overshadowed these attributes. During his campaign, many knew that he was Christian but utilized the lie that he was Muslim as a tactic to scare off voters. Why would it be so bad to have a Muslim leading the country? America had the same phobia about African Americans, now we had an African American President.

Annual Military Charities 2009

Every year all of the branches of the military had a drive for the Combined Federal Campaign or CFC. The mission of the CFC was to support and promote philanthropy through a voluntary program that was employee-focused, cost-efficient and effective in providing all federal employees the opportunity to improve the quality of life for all. Federal employees, who included the military, continued to make the CFC the largest and most successful workplace fundraiser in the world. The national, international and local organizations that fell under the CFC umbrella had been scrutinized to meet the CFC eligibility requirements.

To my knowledge, there were two Islamic organizations that fell under the CFC umbrella and I donated to them every year. Each organization had a small write-up in the CFC brochure that explained what the donations were used for and it explained how much of the donation actually went toward supporting their cause and administration fees. There might have been more Islamic charities out there but you really had to research them. I'm sure that terrorist networks were trying to solicit funds in the United States. The two that I donated to, had websites that showed photos of the organization at work and to which countries their aid was flowing to. If you donated through their site or sent checks or money orders, you could select any country you desired to assist.

As a community in Okinawa, we focused on Chechnya, Bosnia, Ethiopia, and Palestine. We also focused on countries that were hit by natural disasters like Indonesia, Pakistan, and Turkey. After the 9/11 attack, one of the organizations was shut down for a year while the FBI investigated its contribution destinations. Allegedly, the organization was channeling funds to Al-Qaeda. The organization was reopened and continued to provide food, clothing and shelter to many across the globe. I applauded both of these organizations for the work they did and I'm happy that they utilized federal employees and the military as a vessel to make it happen.

Independence Day 2009 in Houston

With my daughter and her family leaving for Okinawa, Japan in a couple weeks, the ladies of the family decided to go to Houston for the 4th of July to see a live performance of one of their favorite artists. While they were at the show, I would visit with a Palestinian family, whose son I met while he was fulfilling his two week Air Force Reserve obligation in Okinawa, Japan.

We left San Antonio for Houston early the morning of the 4th. I called their son that morning to let them know that we were coming. We were in the month of Ramadan so we were fasting during the day. His mother invited us for Iftar (the breaking of the fast) at sunset. We checked into our hotel and the first place the family wanted to go was to the mall. That was usually the first place we went on any trip to a new city. Afterwards, we went to visit the family that I had heard of years ago when I met my now former son-in-law in Okinawa, Japan. He met the family in Houston around 1990 after graduating from boot camp with their son, and they informally adopted him. He even legally changed his last name to theirs. From the conversations I had about the family, I often wondered why and how the family ended up in Houston. I talked with one of the sons and he enlightened me on a little of their family history.

Their father was from the Gaza Strip in Palestine, and their mother was from Jerusalem. That geographical area was well known for its instability due to the Israeli occupation in the 1960s. He excelled in his academics and received a scholarship to Cairo University in Egypt with a focus on Civil Engineering. I was really surprised to hear that his roommate at the university was the former leader of Palestine and the Chairman of the Palestine Liberation Organization (PLO).

After graduating he heard that there was a strong demand for civil engineers in America. He obtained a visa and flew to Chicago to pursue his desire to live in a country without war, turmoil and political strife. He landed a job with a firm and purchased a house. Later he went back to the Middle East to find a wife to start a family. He found a wife at a refugee camp in Jordan and they were soon married. They had the first four of their nine children in Chicago and the other five in Dhahran, Saudi Arabia after having his job transferred. The gas and oil industry led him back to Houston where they now resided.

Of the nine children in the family, three of them were boys. Their father had the deepest respect for the military, especially the U. S. Marines, and he instilled the same respect and admiration in his sons. All three had dreams of becoming U. S. Marines. When the older two sons were of age, he enrolled them in a Marine Military Academy. They both were commissioned and served their time in the Corps. One is now serving in the Air Force Inactive Reserves, with twenty-two years under his belt. The third son enlisted in the Marine Corps and went to Boot Camp with my now former son-in-law. He received his discharge after four years. It was good to know that the five of us shared that common bond that Marines had. That was one attribute that distinguished Marines from the other branches of service.

The family lived in an upscale neighborhood. We arrived at their house and one of the sisters and their mother was there. We all introduced ourselves and we were very pleased to meet each other. They asked where we were staying and we told them at a local hotel. They insisted that we stay at their home, however, our rooms were paid for in advance and it was too late to cancel the reservations. We talked about our families and our future plans. We talked about living in the United States as Muslims and the stereotypical issues that we faced as Muslims from ignorant citizens who knew nothing about Islam and didn't care to know. They also told us how much of a struggle it was living in Palestine, where one of the sisters was living at that time. She was an activist against the Israeli occupation in Gaza, and there had been countless times where her life had been in danger.

While talking, another sister arrived along with another brother and their families. It was soon sunset and time to break our fast. They prepared an enormous feast of food and we didn't know where to begin. Everything looked good as our eyes just wandered from one dish to another. Of course everything was prepared Arab style and we have always had a taste for Arab food. After dinner they served the traditional Arab tea and coffee. We relaxed for a while until it was time for the ladies to get ready for their show. We took them back to the hotel and went back to the family's house to enjoy more of their hospitality.

We engaged in more conversation about Palestine over tea and it definitely gave me a better perspective of the situation there that no one had been able to help both sides rectify. Palestine had become one of the most sensitive issues for Muslims worldwide and until that area was stabilized, world-wide national security would always be jeopardized. We left their house with one of the families to see a fireworks display in the park.

The next morning we were back on the road to San Antonio. I had a flight that evening back to San Diego. Our thanks and gratitude cannot be measured for their outpour of hospitality and fellowship extended to us during our stay in Houston. We only spent a day with them, but it felt like we were actually family. Not only was it a pleasant experience, but it was an educational experience as well. We were also grateful that we were able to share the spirit of Ramadan with them. This was a reflection of what the entire month of Ramadan was about. We looked forward to the opportunity to see them again and Insha Allah (God willing) our next trip would be just as enjoyable.

My Home Away From Home

Aboard the Depot we had what is called the Marine Corps Community Services Recreation Center which was open for operation every day except for some holidays. This establishment was where I spent the majority of my time since arriving in San Diego. Their hours of operation accommodated their patrons and their staff provided a family like atmosphere that was infectious on the Depot. The facility offered an array of things to do inside and it became the focal point or place to be there on the installation. It had a bowling alley, a theater, an Irish Pub, a renowned kitchen and staff, a cyber café, a game room with all free games, free long distance phone calls with a military ID, video games, a bar, and the Locker Room which served as a mini-club for drinks and dancing. The facility was also equipped with over 20 televisions, including flat screens with cable and Direct TV, wireless internet, and a large remote screen television that came in handy for Sunday's NFL games and any other sports events of high visibility. The big screen was also the ticket for the Super Bowl and NBA Finals, along with free food, t-shirts, games and prizes. The facility was also utilized for parties, banquets, seminars, and any other events that required food, a large space for eating and activities that kept children occupied for hours. In addition, it served as a summer camp for children once school was out. They offered an occasional comedy night where they contracted well known comedians, casino nights, and Bingo on Wednesdays. The facility could host just about any request. They often conducted surveys to see what patrons would like to have. Bingo was very popular on the Depot but it was small scale compared to the many local casinos that were doing extremely well. I didn't participate in either of the two nor the Locker Room because the atmospheres of these activities were not conducive to Muslim behavior. Islam taught Muslims to avoid alcohol and gambling with no exceptions. Our Islamic doctrine stated that alcohol and gambling were the handy work of Satan. This had definitely proven to be true. Our jails are filled with individuals that drank and overindulged, especially Marines. Alcohol had been a problem with Marines since its existence and it still plagued the Corps. Regardless of how much we stressed drinking responsively, drinking and driving, and safety, as we still had major issues with alcohol. I've had to explain this many times because my friends noticed that I didn't go into the Locker Room and I didn't play Bingo. Once I explained why, they understood. They respected the religion and most asked questions when they were curious. This really came into play after an incident that happened the first time my wife visited the Depot. The facility was known as a "no hat" zone, meaning that you couldn't wear hats, bandanas, scarves or any type of head coverings inside. My wife was Muslim and she wore the traditional head scarf or hijab inside the building. She was not with me at the time. She was asked by one of the members of the staff to remove her hijab and she told the staff member that she wasn't going to remove it because it was required by her religion to wear. The staff member told her that she would have to ask her boss if my wife could wear it. My wife insisted that she be able to talk with the boss. The staff member then told my wife that it would be alright until she received an answer. My wife proceeded to the cyber café. After she checked her email, she returned to our room and told me that one of the staff in the recreation center asked her to remove her hijab. I told her that they probably didn't know the significance as to why she wore it and that it was probably the first time they encountered something like this. We returned to the center the next day and the same staff member was there, who I knew well. She apologized to my wife and said that she just didn't know the religious significance of the hijab. She didn't reveal whether she had talked to her boss or not but she had a totally different attitude about the situation. I really felt that it was important for employers to educate their employees on religious accommodations and cultural diversity. With scores of immigrants entering this country, it would be an advantage for any organization to implement training in these two areas.

Because it had so much to offer, I chose to make the center my second home while stationed at the Depot. I always looked forward to going over after work just to mingle with the staff or to order one of my favorite meals. If I had nothing planned on weekends, I would spend most of both days there. Marine Corps Community Services did a fantastic job in accommodating its patrons. I knew that I would miss the convenience and hospitality of the Center when my tour was completed. It definitely had an impact on my life.

Damage Control After Ft. Hood

I left San Diego for San Antonio to attend the Marine Corps Ball in Corpus Christi on November 5, 2009. When I arrived in Houston for my layover, I caught a glimpse of the television that was reflecting some breaking news out of Ft. Hood, Texas. Apparently there was an Army Major who went on a shooting spree at one of the family centers on the base. I could only pray that the shooter was not a Muslim, and that this would not be another opportunity for the media to vilify Islam. As I sat down to watch closer they showed the shooter's name and all I could do was shake my head in disgust. From what the media was reporting, the Major was a psychiatrist who was distraught about an upcoming deployment to Afghanistan. The media also reported that the Major also protested the fact that the U. S. Military was operating on Muslim soil overseas. The most critical issue that the media wanted to exploit was how the religion of Islam was responsible for the shooting. I would hate to speculate as to why the Major would act the way he did and only he would be able to say. About thirty days after the shooting, his medical condition still prevented him from speaking. I can say for a fact how unfair and biased the media was when it came to acts of terrorism and the Islamic religion.

During the same time frame, there were two more top stories in the news. One was about a man in Florida that went on a shooting spree and killed five members of his family. The next was a story about a man in Ohio that killed 12 women over a period of years and buried them in his house. These were in fact acts of terrorism. Not one time in either of the stories, and I'm talking through extensive coverage, did the media mention anything about the religion of these two suspects. Not one word of Christianity was aired on national television. On the other hand, as soon as the press received word that the shooter was Muslim or claimed to be Muslim, the religion of Islam was responsible for the shooting. This had been the pattern for quite some time now. Strangely enough, even when Christian groups made the news for committing acts that were prejudicial to the good order and faith of the religion, Christianity was not persecuted like Islam. There were so many incidents like that which have occurred, along with murders and other heinous crimes, committed by Christians, Jews, and members of other faith groups, and the fact that the suspects belonged to one of these faiths was not mentioned. Whenever a Muslim, or one who claimed to be Muslim but committed un-Islamic acts was involved in something like this, Islam was always the blame. There were over 1.5 billion Muslims in the world so don't you think that if this is what the religion taught, wouldn't we have a lot more shootings and bombings?

Now that the incident had occurred, the Muslims that properly represented the religion were being persecuted by the backlash of threats, discrimination, and abuse from societies all over the world. I don't know if these suspects thought about what would happen to innocent Muslims if these acts were carried out, or what would be the consequences for their friends and family. I really didn't think that it was fair because so many of us worked so hard at giving people the true picture of Islam through peace and understanding. The reporters spoke with Islamic leaders across the nation and they all condemned the shooting. This had little effect on how Islam was still being portrayed in the media.

Whenever in the company of friends, family, or strangers and I had the opportunity to speak about Islam I took advantage of it. That was one thing that we as Muslims could have done to educate non-Muslims about the true teachings of Islam. The knowledge was not going to come from any other source but us. With fanaticism becoming more popular throughout the world, educating the public would play a major part in our defense.

A True Humanitarian

On December 10, 2009, my colleague and my boss were invited to a luncheon in one of the most exclusive areas in San Diego, La Jolla. They, along with military members from the area bases, were attending a luncheon, primarily geared toward women and commanders, to hear a gentleman speak who had dedicated the last sixteen years of his life toward educating and empowering children, particularly girls. Seats for the luncheon were paid for by local organizations and this was why the luncheon was invitation only and not open to the public. That morning as they prepped to leave for the luncheon, I called around the command to see if anyone else was able to attend. My colleague sent me his website and I read about his accomplishments and awards through his biography. I really wanted to attend because the type of work that the gentleman was doing had touched the hearts of so many people all over the world. I personally wanted to hear about his experience and what motivated him to sacrifice so much of his life helping others. After calling around to see if anyone could attend, I went back to his website to see if he was conducting any more presentations and book autographs. The site showed that he had another presentation directly after the luncheon, and was having one that night at a local church, sponsored by Warick's Bookstore. I made the intentions then to attend.

When my colleague returned from the luncheon that afternoon, she presented me with an autographed copy of 'Three Cups of Tea,' The Younger Reader's Edition that was followed up by the adult's edition, 'Stones Into Schools.' She told me about the exclusive crowd at the presentation and its contents. She reflected that there were incidents mentioned in the presentation that brought tears to her eyes. I really looked forward to attending that evening so that I could hear for myself from a true humanitarian.

I arrived at the Unity Center a half hour before the presentation and I was overwhelmed by the number of people that were attending. As I approached the crowded door, I heard the gentleman standing there asking for tickets. This presented a problem because I didn't know that you had to have tickets to enter. I asked if I could purchase a ticket at the door and he said that the presentation was completely sold out, and that the center was at its capacity. He asked if I wanted to come into the lobby to purchase a book and I told him that I did.

While purchasing my book, a wonderful woman who overheard my conversation with the gentleman at the door came over and asked if I needed a ticket. I replied "Yes," and she said, "Hold on One Minute," smiling. She went to the door and began asking people if they had extra tickets as they walked in. I heard another wonderful woman say that her husband bailed out at the last minute so she had an extra ticket. The woman pointed at me and said that I needed a ticket. I quickly stated that I would purchase the ticket from her. While exchanging the money for the ticket, the woman told me that she thought that it was wonderful that it was mandatory for all military commanders to read 'Three Cups of Tea' and its sequel 'Stones Into Schools.' I told her that I agreed. Out of nowhere, she then told me to take the $15 back and said, "Thanks for serving our country." I didn't know what to say. I insisted that she keep the money but she waved it off and told me to enjoy the presentation.

As I walked into the presentation area, I saw that my next task was to find a seat. As I looked around for an empty seat, a woman approached me and asked if I needed a seat. She directed me to a row with one empty seat in the middle. I squeezed my way through the aisle to the seat. As I looked around the room, I noticed that I was the only African American in the room. I thought that I might have been the only Muslim in the crowd but it looked to be a Pakistani family that sat in front of me. Prior to introducing the guest speaker, they acknowledged a group of VIP donors that gave large sums of money for the guest speaker's cause. They also acknowledged a group of elementary school children, their teacher, and principal that traveled from Orange County, two hours away, to attend the presentation. The children presented the guest speaker with a $4000.00 check for his organization Pennies for Peace.

The guest speaker looked totally different from what I had seen on his website. In all of the pictures I had previously seen of him, he was dressed in a traditional Afghan or Pakistani shalwar khamees. That night he had on a sport jacket. He was making an attempt to climb the second highest mountain in the world known as K2, and on his way down he wandered into a village and saw some children who he first thought were playing in the dirt. They actually had sticks and were writing in the dirt. Shockingly, he realized that this was their school. He made a promise to the children that he would return to Pakistan and build them a school and he did just that. In fact, he built a total of 130 schools between the remote areas of Pakistan and Afghanistan. Primarily focusing on schools for girls, his philosophy was if you educated girls and women, you're educating the entire community. In much of Afghanistan and Pakistan, women were deprived of education. Although these were both Muslim countries, this was totally against the teachings of Islam. The first word revealed from Allah (swt) to the Prophet Muhammad (Pbuh), was "Iqra," or "Read," and according to the Prophet Muhammad (Pbuh), that applied to women also. Even though he had been threatened and captured by the Taliban, he still made education a priority for the deprived children of these countries. He escaped from the Taliban after a week of captivity. In addition to pursuing education for the children of the region, another of his goals was to promote peace through education. By educating the communities, he was winning the hearts of the communities that realized the importance of education for the future of their countries. Many of the elders or leaders of these communities built close ties with him that had helped our ground forces better understand the Taliban and the culture. This was one of the key reasons why his books had become mandatory reading material for all commanders with future plans of deploying to the region.

After the presentation, they announced that the speaker would be signing autographs in the lobby and that the autograph sections would correspond to the alphabetical letters on our tickets. My ticket had a "D," which would be the last section. There were over 600 people attending and the line had already formed for the first section. If I waited for an autograph, it would've taken me hours to get out of there that night. I sat there in my chair and started to contemplate if I should just leave or wait the three hours for an autographed book. Suddenly, I felt a tap on my shoulder and I heard someone say, "Thank you for coming, can I sign your book?" It was the guest speaker! I gave him my book and he asked what my name was. I asked if he could write "As Salaam Alaikum," (Peace be Unto You) in the book and he included it with my name. He handed me the book and I thanked him in Farsi, "Momnoon." The speaker learned three languages while living in the region and Persian was one of them.

I noticed that after the presentation he stepped off the stage but I had no idea which direction he went. The next thing I know, he was behind me. It was a great experience attending the presentation, especially after considering the facts that when I arrived, I didn't have a ticket, didn't think I would find a seat, and I thought I'd have to wait all night for an autograph.

Two days after the show I told one of my close Muslim families about the guest speaker and the wonderful work he had done in both countries. They asked if he was Muslim and if he wasn't, did he have a hidden agenda behind the work that he was doing. The usual pitch is that Christians went into Muslim countries and provided some type of assistance but their main intent is to convert the Muslims to Christianity. This led me to conduct more research on the guest speaker. I read through both of his books to look for signs or key words that would lead me to believe that he was a missionary of some sort. I checked all three of his sites for further clues. I even explored Google and Yahoo as a last resort.

I recognized that he had been awarded the highest civil award in Pakistan, the Star of Pakistan. There was no doubt in my mind that if he was trying to convert Muslims to Christianity, the Islamic Leaders, Tribal Chiefs, and the Taliban would have marked him for death. I truly think that he was a true humanitarian with good intentions, and that he didn't have a hidden agenda behind his work. He was also a co-founder of the Central Asia Institute and founder of Pennies of Peace, two organizations that had received world-wide accolades for their contributions to his cause. I haven't mentioned his name in the book, but he was recently nominated for the Nobel Peace Prize and there is not one person on this earth that deserved it more.

At the Mercy of the Taliban

On February 5, 2010, I attended Friday prayers at the Islamic Center of San Diego. After the prayers, they handed out flyers to attend a fund raiser to raise funds for the Muslim Legal Fund of America. There was a brother from this area who was jailed for his alleged involvement with a Palestinian Terrorist group and most of the proceeds would be utilized to offset his legal fees. The guest speaker for the evening would be a former hard-drinking, hard-nosed British female journalist who was sent to Afghanistan two weeks after 9/11 to write a story on our President's "War on Terror." Her paper, the British Sunday Express, shuttled her into Islamabad, Pakistan and she disguised herself in a burka and tried to make it through a Taliban check-point, in an attempt to gain entry into Afghanistan. While going through the check-point, her donkey was spooked and threw her off, exposing her camera to a Taliban soldier. Being aware of the brutal treatment toward women that the Taliban exercised, she immediately thought that she would be stoned, gang-raped or beaten. She had prayed that she would die quickly.

She was jailed in Jalalabad and then was transported to the capital Kabul. Contrary to what she had heard and seen of the Taliban, they treated her rather well. I quote this from her diary, "They constantly referred to me as their guest and say that they are sad if I am sad. I can't believe it. I wish everyone at home knew how I was being treated. I bet people think I am being tortured, beaten and sexually abused. Instead, I am being treated with kindness and respect. It is unbelievable."

She recalled a funny story about her Taliban captors. Two days prior to a serious NATO Forces bombing on the Taliban, she decided to wash her underwear and hung them on the prison washing line to dry. The captors asked her to take them down and she refused. They had to send the Taliban Deputy Foreign Minister to convince her to take them down. He stated that the community would have impure thoughts about the captors. Here they were, two days from being bombed, and they were more concerned about the community having dirty thoughts about them because of the hanging underwear.

The British journalist was held for ten days and was only released when she promised her captors that she would read the Quran and study about Islam. Once she returned to the United Kingdom, she turned to the

Quran in an effort to better understand her captors and experience. The Church of England Sunday school teacher was blown away by what she read. Furthermore, she was intrigued that not one word has been changed in the Quran since its existence. The Quran changed her life. Less than two years after her captivity, the English journalist became Muslim.

When she was asked about the place of women in Islam, she replied, "There are oppressed women in Muslim countries, but I can take you up the side streets of Tyneside, United Kingdom, and show you oppressed women there. Oppression is cultural, it is not Islamic. The Quran makes it clear that women are equal." She went on to add that her new Muslim dress was empowering. She reflected that it was very liberating to be judged for her mind and not the size of her bust or length of her legs.

After her three marriages, Islam transformed her from a woman who would wait by the phone for a man to ring, to a woman who no longer had to worry about it. I quote her again, "I have no man stress. For the first time since my teens I don't have that pressure to have a boyfriend or husband."

When her contract expired with the Sunday Press, she was hired by Al-Jazeera, an Arab News Station in Doha, Qatar as a Senior Editor of its English-language website. She worked with the station for about six months and was later terminated by a contract dispute. She has since been a committed Peace Campaigner, and a strong advocate against the war strategy in Afghanistan, citing that "bombs and bullets are not necessarily the answer."

She had become an Islamic Feminist who promoted women's rights and would take advantage of every opportunity to defend all women. A staunch supporter of the niqab, the face veil revealing only the eyes, she rejects disparaging comments made by the former Secretary and the Government Ministers of Britain that the niqab only serves as a barrier for communication. Muslim women saw the niqab and burka as political symbols as well as religious requirements. She noted an embarrassing and degrading moment when the emergence of Miss Afghanistan in a bikini was hailed as a giant leap for women's liberation in Afghanistan. "The western-world, along with the countries who were misguided by it, had totally missed the mark when it comes to women of righteousness. Superiority in Islam is accomplished through piety, not beauty, wealth, power, position, sex, or the ability or desire of a woman to take off her clothes."

Another Muslim Chaplain

In October of 2009, I received a phone call from a brother who had received my number from a former Navy Muslim Chaplain who I served with in Okinawa, Japan. The former Chaplain was now living in California. The brother who called was preparing to be the next Navy Muslim Chaplain. At that time he was going through training in Quantico, Virginia. He called to ask if he could give my name and number to a gentleman at Virginia Commonwealth University who was writing a documentary about Muslims in the military. He had already been interviewed and he thought that with my time in the military, I would have some valuable information to share for the project. A week later I received a call from the gentleman at VCU and he asked when we could do a telephonic interview. Because it was a documentary, I wanted to clear it through my Public Affairs Office before I agreed to do the interview. My Public Affairs Office at the Depot had to clear it through the Headquarters, U.S. Marine Corps Public Affairs Office.

The brother also told me that he had no idea where his detailer would station him after he completed his training. At that time, the Navy had three Muslim Chaplains on active duty; one was at the Pentagon in D. C., one was at the Great Lakes in Illinois, and the other was located in Okinawa, Japan. We stated that it would be good to have some Islamic representation on the West Coast. In February of 2010, I received a call from the brother and he was right here on the Depot going through two weeks training with our Chaplains. He told me that he would come by my office to finally meet me face to face. He came by my office the following day. That coming Friday we attended Friday prayers at the Islamic Center of San Diego and then had lunch at my favorite restaurant Bismillah. He explained that he wanted to be a Chaplain because there was a need for representing Islam in its true light. He further stated that it was a unique opportunity to serve God, country, and his creation all at the same time.

We also talked about his background and how it was growing up in Kuwait as a native Indian. His parents migrated from Bombay, India and his father worked as an Engineer at the Kuwait Oil Company. The Chaplain's family was actually in Kuwait when Iraqi Forces invaded in

1990. The invasion caused his family to evacuate back to Bombay until the conflict had subsided. Although the Chaplain was born and raised in Kuwait, he studied Petroleum Engineering at Montana Technical Institute in Butte, Montana and then enlisted in the Navy. With his degree almost completed, he pursued the opportunity to become a Chaplain. He experienced some procedural issues with his application but with the help of the Navy Muslim Chaplain at the Washington Navy Yard in D. C., who we both knew, he was able to overcome his adversities.

From my conversations with the other Muslim Chaplains and fellow military Muslims, it was imperative that we had the Muslim Chaplains on active duty. What most military personnel fail to realize is that Muslims Chaplains serve in the same capacity as our other Chaplains; they're not just for the Muslims. They underwent the same training as our traditional Chaplains. With the conflicts in Iraq and Afghanistan, both predominately Muslim countries, our commanders could utilize their expertise and guidance to our advantage. From what we've seen thus far, it had paid dividends. I recall in Okinawa where the Commanding General would utilize the Muslim Chaplain there to travel to countries like Malaysia and Indonesia to meet the country's leadership prior to U. S. forces deploying there for joint exercises. He would then return to Okinawa, provide classes and lectures on the customs and courtesies of the respective countries and deploy with the forces. Ground Commanders were now using the Muslim leadership in Afghanistan as allies against the Taliban. Good relationships with the local Mullahs and Elders were now a key to the success of ridding the country of the extremist Taliban.

The Chaplain was recently commissioned and had been assigned to Marine Corps Base at Camp Pendleton, California. I looked forward to talking with him and sharing some of his experiences as a unit Chaplain. Many of the units were preparing to deploy from Camp Pendleton and I knew that it was only a matter of time before his unit would be committed to help fight the "War on Terrorism" in Afghanistan.

A Native Perspective on Somalia

On April 19, 2010, my fascination of cultures led me to attend a lecture and book signing of a well known sister from the Somali community. The lecture took place in the third floor Culture Exhibit of the downtown San Diego Library. The sister had written a book about the experiences of the Somali Refugees that had fled to the United States due to the civil war that had disrupted the stability of Somalia. She gave first hand accounts of what her family experienced and she read a couple of passages from the book. The book was written through the eyes of a fictional character named Nadifo who married a prominent Foreign Minister and moved to Minnesota. Minnesota now maintained one of the largest Somali communities in the United States.

During her lecture, she stated that she had been in the United States for five years and had entered through the nation's capital, Washington, D.C. It took her three years to complete the book and she mentioned the controversial nature of the text. Some of her people, including family, did not agree with some of the information she had disclosed about her country and some agreed with her wholeheartedly. What I found interesting was the fact that the Somali culture had been well known and publicized for their contributions to poetry but their work was not being circulated throughout the globe. Furthermore, no other person of Somali descent had attempted to write about the Somali refugee experience and she wanted to be the first to tell her own story and not hear it from someone else. Her desire was to be the first to capture that limelight.

When I asked what inspired her to write the book, she replied that it was the events that took place after September 11, 2001 and the fact that the western media always portrayed Somali women as being oppressed. She wanted to convey to the misinformed that the large majority of her people were peaceful and dedicated to the true teachings of Islamic principles, and not supportive to what was experienced at the World Trade Center, nor the recent events of the Somali pirates hijacking ships in the Indian Ocean and the Gulf of Aden and holding the crews for ransom. She repeatedly said that life for Somali women was hard because of their domestic duties but they were given the same opportunities for career development as most women.

Having the desire and compassion to write her book was a blessing for her and needless to say, it served as a remedy for her mental frustration from dealing with the civil, political, and economical issues of her country. She was not proud of what was going on in Somalia and the book served as therapeutic treatment for her. Writing the book gave her a sense of tranquility and when completed, an overwhelming sense of accomplishment and pride.

It was a mental challenge to complete the book and, sadly, at it's completion she could not find any takers to publish it. She tried the traditional approach but to no avail. Straight forward and determined, she found an editor on line for about $4,000.00, and she published the book herself, totaling about $15,000.00. On a good note, one of the local professors stated that he would make the book mandatory reading for his students at the University of San Diego.

While accompanied by her husband, the sister brought books in to autograph and sell. This was another book that I looked forward to reading and later stashing in my home library. There was so much that I didn't know but wanted to know about Somali culture. What better source could I use to gain a broader knowledge on one of the most misunderstood countries in present days?

Each of the experiences that I have mentioned in this book have touched me in some way and may have had an impact on how some may look at the Islamic faith. From my writings, some will take away a wealth of knowledge and some will take what they have read and will remain closed-minded to the opportunity to learn about the fastest growing religion on the planet. From a military perspective, which definitely embraces the idea of sharing an intimate relationship with God, service members have become more open-minded about the religion probably because of their experiences in Muslim countries, and their affiliation with military Muslims here in the states and abroad. Due to this affiliation, many have embraced Islam as their way of life. I often wondered if their experiences had been as enjoyable as mine had been. With the exception of two or three bad experiences, the majority of my experiences while being a Muslim in the military have had a positive impact in my life and many of those friends and family that I have been in contact with.

Jummah (Friday Prayers)

I always looked forward to Friday because it was our day of worship. I went into work and ensured that my critical issues were taken care of before I left around 11:30 p.m. to attend. My bosses knew my routine and didn't have a problem with me working half days on Friday. If there were pressing issues, I would return to work after prayers. The Quran told us to leave work on Fridays to attend prayers and then return to work afterwards. Jummah was a mandatory religious obligation for men but the women are excused because of their responsibilities at the home. Most attended anyway because they realized the importance of praying in congregation. Jummah had been so crowded at Masjid Abu Bakr (Islamic Center of San Diego) that they had to have a second service. The first started at 12:15 p.m. and the second at 1:15 p.m. I arrived around 11:50 p.m. like clockwork and I parked at the same place to avoid the traffic after Jummah was over. As I parked I saw Muslims walking from each direction from the nearby neighborhoods where they resided. The crosswalks leading to the masjid were full around this time as the stop-lights halted the traffic.

Walking into the masjid was so soothing. It felt good to get away from the hustle and bustle of typical Friday business and traffic. The quiet and peaceful state of the masjid gave me the opportunity to reflect on the blessings that Allah (swt) had bestowed on my family and I from the last Jummah. It was quiet inside other than the repeating of the traditional greeting of peace, "As Salaam Alaikum" (Peace be unto you) that you would hear when brothers greeted each other. Accompanied by the greeting would be a kiss to both cheeks or a hug, depending on which ethnic group you belonged to. You also heard the low murmur of brothers reading the Quran or just having conversation. The walls of the masjid were simple and bare, unlike traditional churches with distractive photos and symbols in plain view. On occasion, you would hear the sisters and babies upstairs who prayed separately from the men. After praying my two rakahs, I either read the Quran or made thikr until the Imam or Khateeb started the khutbah or sermon. Thikr meant remembering and we'd say "Thikr Allah," or "remembering God." We did this by repeating "Subhanah Allah" (Glory is to God), and "Alhamdulilah" (All praise is to God) thirty-three times, and "Allahu Ahkbar" (God is the Greatest) thirty-four times. Thikr was repeated over and over.

When I didn't read or make thikr, I watched as the brothers walked in to find places to sit. By the time I arrived, the front row of the masjid was already filled from one side to the other. This was the first row that would stand behind the Imam or Khateeb as he led the prayer. There was an abundance of blessings for those who arrived to the masjid early enough to get the front row. I always took my seat along the side wall to support my back. The same brothers usually sat next to me. I watched as fathers would bring their children in. I would even witness sons bringing their fathers in or older relatives who needed to sit in chairs instead of sitting on the floor as we did in the masjid. Even as the Khateeb gave the khutbah, there were Muslims still walking in trying to find a place to sit amongst the near capacity congregation. Many were always forced to sit at the entrance in the hallway by the shoe racks. Many would rather sit there to avoid the congestion after prayer was over.

Once the Imam started the khutbah, you didn't hear a sound except for his voice or an occasional cough or throat clearing. In Islam you were not permitted to talk while the khutbah is being conducted. Everyone was focused on the message that the Imam delivered. Once the khutbah concluded and the Imam conducted the prayer, it was like an exodus of bodies heading back to work, home, or to carry out the rest of their day. Many often came back to the masjid for the next three prayers because of the benefits of prayer in congregation and being in the masjid.

On the way out after prayer I looked into the kitchen on the right and I watched as the cooks prepared and served meals for those who decided to feed their appetite before leaving. The plates of rice, bread, chicken or beef were sold for five dollars a plate with the proceeds being given back to the masjid. I always made it routine to stop at the masjid store on the way out. It maintained a large inventory of Middle-Eastern foods, clothing, books, and treats for the children that had them dragging their parents in to browse. Outside of the masjid was the area where everyone congregated to talk with those who they hadn't seen all week. I looked for the Moroccan group that I usually talked with but they might have headed back to work and school already. This was also the area where vendors would take advantage of empty hands of passers-by and handed out flyers advertising their businesses. It seemed like every week there were more Muslim stores and restaurants opening. San Diego had become a Muslim haven for business. Most of the time, I would venture to my favorite restaurant after Jummah and I would often see that other Muslims had the same idea because they would follow suit.

I left the masjid with a feeling of spiritual enlightenment as I always did when I attended Jummah. Again it was time to go into my day-to-day routine and put into practice the lesson that was passed by the Imam that reflected the character and morals of the Prophet Muhammad (Pbuh) and his Sahabah, or the Muslims that surrounded him. It was always a challenge for me to maintain good Muslim character in a Marine environment where most of the casual conversations centered around alcohol, women, partying, and other subjects that made one think that our society was not even conscientious of religious lifestyles. I thank Allah (swt) that I was different and that I'll continue to show my friends and colleagues that Islam is the answer to the problems we have in our society. I went back to the office to check on hot issues and then to the recreation center for dinner.

Do or Die; The Ultimatum in Combat

During the course of my career after becoming Muslim in 1994, I've been asked by several inquiring minds if I wanted to go to combat and if I did, would I kill another Muslim. At the time of Operation Iraqi Freedom in 1991, I was stationed at the Military Entrance Processing Station (MEPS) in Newark, New Jersey and I wasn't a Muslim. A couple of the Marines stationed with me wanted to go but we were restricted from leaving MEPS duty because of the need to process incoming service members due to the conflict. Since Operation Enduring Freedom began in 2001, I've been asked and each time I gave the same answer.

With so many rumors you hear about how bad Marines want to go to war, I on the other hand feel that in most cases, war can and should be avoided by all means. If the leaders involved can eliminate politics, greed, and hidden agendas, most conflicts can be resolved peacefully without bloodshed. I felt that U. S. presence in Iraq, besides the invasion of Kuwait was based on a lie and was unnecessary. I do believe, however, our presence in Afghanistan was warranted by the need to combat terrorism. I would never volunteer to go to war but if ordered I would go in to carry out the mission. If I was faced with the situation of protecting my life or the lives of the Marines and Sailors around me, I would have no other course of action but to take the life of an enemy combatant. I can relate to the dilemma of either kill or be killed. If I didn't, then I would die or one of my Marines or Sailors would. In the military I am sworn to an oath that states that "I will protect my country against all enemies, foreign and domestic." Marines take that oath very seriously.

I can also relate to the fact that with my military occupational specialty (MOS), Administration, the chance of me actually experiencing a situation like that was slim to none. What I learned from talking to Marines that had experienced those situations was that most of them had combat related jobs that frequently put them in the face of danger. They also shared that taking the life of another human being could have a devastating effect on a person mentally. Post Traumatic Stress Disorder (PTSD) was one of the highest concerns from our service members returning from Iraq and Afghanistan. The sight of death had changed the lives of many, along with their families, who had experienced combat. Although combat might serve as a measuring stick for those who want to test their courage, the after effects of combat seemed to demonstrate that the cost of protecting our freedom was taking its toll.

Bible Belt Islamophobia

Today, July 30, 2010, I attended Friday prayers at the Islamic Center. At the conclusion of the prayers, the Imam made a special announcement that at the Temecula Masjid, about 45 minutes away, a group of Christians were burning Holy Qurans outside of the masjid announcing their "International Burn a Koran Day," which was to take place on the 9th anniversary of the 9/11 attacks in the United States. They were also lining the sidewalks with their dogs because they heard that Muslims didn't like dogs. Muslims only kept dogs as outdoor pets because of their filthy nature. We prayed on the floor and dogs had habits that were unsanitary. This was done in an effort to chase Muslims away from attending the masjid for Friday prayers. This was initiated by a southern Christian hate group from Gainesville, Florida that claimed that Islam was the religion of the devil. The Imam asked if we could join a peaceful protest against the ill-advised group.

C.A.I.R., (The Council for American Islamic Relations) and other Christian groups committed to showing their support for the masjid. CAIR, the largest Islamic advocacy group, responded to the hate group by encouraging Muslims world-wide to host "Share the Quran" dinners with non-Muslims to help them learn more about the religion. Being in the military, I was not allowed to participate in protests of this nature. The protest was peaceful and uneventful.

Although the Christian group thought that they were helping to tarnish the reputation of Islam, they were actually helping to promote it. With so much talk in the media about the Muslim world, the people who are not familiar with Islam were becoming more curious about the religion. This led them to start researching different aspects of the religion. Just as it was noted after 9/11, Islam grew at a rapid rate. It was shown again that once people researched the religion and realized its true teachings, they became Muslims. The same situation happened after the start of the Iraq War.

Prior to the war, the American people were not too familiar with Islam. Once our service members were exposed to the religion while deployed, they widely accepted it. Case and point, I know a Moroccan brother here in San Diego who just moved to Tijuana, Mexico. Along with Arabic and French, he spoke fluent Spanish. After spending a month in Tijuana, he told us that the Catholics there had an enormous thirst for Islam. There too the people were accepting Islam, and this was with all of the negative publicity that they constantly hear about Islam.

I recently watched an interview on the "Deen Show," an Islamic radio and television show about a sister who recently reverted to Islam. Although she had reached a significant level of education studying Christianity, she didn't agree with some of the doctrine. Yes, even after nearly four years of Seminary school, she still had doubts about the concept of the Trinity, Jesus (Pbuh) being God, the legitimacy of the Gospels, and other concepts that most Christians just accepted without rationally thinking about them. She was no longer content with just going along with the program.

Additionally, as a Christian religious leader, she felt the need to learn about Islam and it was then when her calling came clear. With the help of a Syrian sister who translated Arabic for her and answered her questions, Islam became her focus and way of life. She was quick to mention that the Syrian sister did not try to revert her to Islam. After being taught the pillars of Islam, the principles, and the articles of faith, she found it hard not to accept Islam.

She was pursuing a Master's of Divinity from a seminary school in Illinois and abruptly reverted to Islam. She was removed from the school and she lost her job because of her decision, much like many others when they decided to change their faith. She did although obtain her Master's of Divinity.

With the rate that Islam had continued to grow, some Christian leaders were becoming more concerned. It really seemed as if they were starting to get desperate in finding ways to deface Muslims and to give the religion a bad name. Instead of trying to build a mutual relationship with Muslims through dialogue, they were resulting to unnecessary hate tactics that continued to show the world that some American Christians didn't practice what they preached.

Ramadan 2010

Our first day of Ramadan started on Wednesday, the 11th day of August. For the past three Jummahs (Friday prayers), the Imam had been trying to prepare the Ummah (community) mentally and physically for the days of fasting and the lengthy nightly Tarawee prayers, standing, bowing, and prostrating as commanded by our Lord. The Imam also conveyed during his khutbahs (sermons) that in order to receive the full benefits from Ramadan, we had to totally submerge ourselves in worship, exemplifying excellent character, showing kindness to those we came into contact with, and increasing our generosity, especially charity to those who were less fortunate than us. The fasting of Ramadan was tough enough, going fifteen hours without food or drink, breaking our fast at 7:37 p.m., and then to start the Tarawee prayers at 9:15 p.m. During Ramadan, it was recommended that we read the entire Quran on our own during the 30 day period. The Quran was revealed to the Prophet Muhammad (Pbuh) during that month so it was symbolic that we read it. It was also recommended that we stand in congregation while the Quran was being recited. The Quran was divided into 30 parts and a part was read each night during the prayers. That led to long periods of standing while your back ached and your toes went to sleep. I've stood through Tarawee prayers where I've actually had dizzy spells and had to sit down. That was when I was training for the Naha Marathon during Ramadan in Okinawa. Those who are unable to withstand the prolong periods of standing, chairs were provided for them. The month of Ramadan was a very tough month for us and you had to prepare yourself mentally and physically in order to make it successfully. From my previous conversations with Christians about how hard their fasting was, we could only wish that ours was that easy. Abstaining from eating for five hours and being allowed to drink or not watching television for a few hours seems like mere child's play compared to what we're used to.

My first day of Ramadan went well. Physically I felt weak until time to break the fast but I was able to maintain. I was a little skeptical after breaking the fast because I still had to attend Tarawee prayers and didn't know how long we would be standing while the first 1/30th of the Quran was being recited. Since my years of fasting, I've always had to explain to my friends and co-workers how and why we fasted. They truly understood why but many of them respond in a way to say that there is no possible way that they could do it. We fasted because we were commanded to do so in the Quran and furthermore, we fasted so that we could feel and relate to what it was like to go without food and water like many of the unfortunate around the world. By doing this, we built a compassion to help those who were in need.

The first night of Tarawee prayers actually was not bad and I left the masjid that night in total amazement. Although we started at 9:15 p.m., and ended at 10:50 p.m., I was totally overwhelmed by the fact that the brother that recited the Quran that night recited the entire first 1/30th without the Quran. He was one of the inspired, blessed, and admired Muslims that had memorized the entire Quran. We called them "Hafith" in Quran. Hafith in Arabic means "Preserver." Most of them started learning the Quran at special schools called madrassas at around four years old. Surprisingly and only by the grace of Allah (swt), we had teenagers that were "Hafith" in Quran, and they competed annually to share their talents. I can confidently say that there is no other religion that puts more emphasis on preserving their holy scripture than the Muslims. I was a Christian for 34 years and I never recall anyone of that faith that had memorized one page of the Bible.

I shared my first official Iftar of Ramadan 2010 with my Moroccan family. An Iftar is the dinner when you break the fast and it began promptly at sunset. Believe me, after a day of fasting, you didn't want to wait one minute after sunset. It started with dates and milk or water. Traditionally, that was the way that the Prophet Muhammad (Pbuh) broke his fast. We referred to it as "a part of his Sunnah," or his way. Next, we had an assortment of traditional Moroccan dishes, along with soup. I can't remember the names of any of the dishes but I found myself going back for seconds on everything, as did everyone else. For dessert we had a large bowl of watermelon and grapes. After dessert we prayed the sunset prayer. Then, to settle our food we had traditional Moroccan mint tea and that, I could drink all night. At 9:00 p.m. we left for the masjid to attend Tarawee prayers until about 11:00 p.m. We came back to the house and another meal was prepared. It was another traditional Moroccan meal served from one large bowl with olives, potatoes, chicken, onions, and a host of Moroccan spices. We all ate from one bowl, dipping our bread into the dish with our fingers.

My San Diego Ramadan was interrupted by an unexpected trip to Okinawa. My daughter in the Air Force took the option of leaving the Air Force due to hardship as a result of having a child born there, along with my ten year old granddaughter, without the support of her abandoning husband. I was going over solely as support for her. The entire family was excited about our first grandson, that she had named three months before he was due to be born. **Idris Naim Siddiq Camp** would probably be the most spoiled kid on the planet.

After my wife purchased my ticket, I notified my friends and Muslim family there to let them know that I was coming. They began planning for our reunion. With the price of the ticket, I figured that I would catch the scheduled military flight back to Seattle via the Air Mobility Command (AMC), and then catch a commercial flight back to San Diego. The AMC flights flew to many of the military bases and to some international airports free of charge. If there was a cost for a few locations, it was minimal. The flights left Okinawa every Saturday with stopovers in Iwakuni and Yokota, Japan, and Osan, Korea. We've traveled the AMC flights many times and it's been a good experience thus far. Besides, it would be great not to fork out another $1200.00 for a return ticket.

My ten hour trip from Los Angeles to Tokyo, Narita was not as agonizing as I thought it would be. My back didn't tighten up and I didn't experience any muscle spasms as I had done before on long flights. It provided me with ample time to catch up on my writing and to stay ahead of my Quran reading. A couple of movies also helped to pass the time. I arrived in Tokyo around 4:30 p.m. and processed through immigration. I grabbed my luggage and proceeded to the Japan Air Lines (JAL) check-in counter to receive my boarding pass for the last leg of my travel to Okinawa. My flight left at 7:35 p.m. to arrive in Okinawa at 10:30 p.m. For the many trips that I have made from Mainland, Japan to Okinawa, it had never taken three hours to reach the tiny island southward. It was revealed later during the flight that pilots fly slower now to preserve fuel. I remember that in earlier years, it would only take an hour and a half.

During the flight, I was able to doze off a couple times for about fifteen or twenty minutes. We arrived about ten minutes early and I enjoyed viewing the island lights during our approach as I always did each time I arrived on island at night. After I collected my baggage, my daughter arrived and we rode back to Kadena Air Force Base through the lighted city of Naha and then Chatan. I thought about stopping at one of my favorite restaurants for a bite but it was much too late to eat. We made our way through the front gate of the base and on to her residence located in base quarters. Due to the time change and jetlag, I didn't sleep that night, but knew that later that week I would find myself struggling to keep my eyes open.

Early the next morning, my daughter said that she was experiencing some unusual bleeding. We both thought that it was time for her to have the baby. Idris was not due for another month. I gathered my thoughts and off we were to Labor and Delivery at the hospital. I had obtained my international driver's license in San Diego so I was able to drive her. Although I was paranoid about driving on the correct side of the road, I managed to safely arrive at the hospital which was only ten minutes away. I had to get used to driving on the left side of the road again. My daughter called ahead to alert the Labor and Delivery staff that she was on the way. She checked in at the front desk and in she went to her room. The doctor monitored my daughter's blood pressure and the baby's heartbeat for about five hours and decided to let her go home. It was a false alarm but you never know when the actual time would occur.

Later that afternoon, we were out and about reuniting with my old Japanese colleagues and friends, along with the local Muslim community. As we drove down Highway 58, one of the main highways that ran through Okinawa, I reflected back on the days that I drove to and from work, back and forth to the Naha Airport, and just traveling throughout the island visiting various places. My wife and I had the conversation many times about how nice it would be to live in Okinawa. If it wasn't for the fact that our mothers were getting up there in age, Okinawa would've been a possible retirement location.

My first stop was to visit the brother from Iran that owned the car dealerships. His lot was located just outside the base. It was good to see him again, along with one of his sidekicks from Detroit. He hadn't changed a bit since I saw him before we left in 2008. He still had a good sense of humor and he immediately began to exercise it after we asked about each other's families. He was also famous for telling us about some of his experiences growing up in Iran and comparing those experiences to situations occurring there on island.

Next, we were down to Naha City to see my good brother from Yemen with the car dealerships. He wasn't there when we arrived but his worker called him very quickly. He was in the vicinity and returned to his office to meet us. We both traded news about our families and future plans. He told me how successful his business had been and how expensive it was maintaining the business and buying property there for his children. He also told me about an experience he had while traveling from Japan to Houston, Texas. Although he had lived in Okinawa for over 20 years, he never applied for a Japanese passport, which left him with only his passport from Yemen. When he arrived at the stateside immigration counter, the agents with the Transportation Safety Agency (TSA) noticed his Yemen passport and that started a wave of questions. Needless to say, they kept him so long for questions that he missed his connecting flight. Unfortunately, Yemen had gained the reputation of a terrorist country and TSA was not about to take any chances on having their security breached. Obtaining a Japanese passport went high on his priority list because he talked about moving out to San Antonio in about five years. From Naha we went to Camp Foster to visit some of my Japanese friends that I promised to pay a visit while there. Most them I saw, and those who were not in, I would see on my next trip after retirement.

Although I broke my fast on my day of travel, the day after arriving I was back in full swing. I was invited to lunch by my Japanese friends but I had to explain to them why I couldn't eat or drink. They understood from the previous Ramadans I spent there. Every night that I was on island, we were invited to an Iftar, and we broke bread at three of my favorite restaurants, one Indian, one Turkish, and the other Iranian. All three were well worth the two year wait. On my last night there, we were invited by our Pakistani family in Naha for another round of Pakistani food and chai tea with milk. We left there barely able to keep our eyes open because we were so full. We also had the pleasure of spending some quality time with the family. I met the brother from Pakistan back in 1995, while deployed to Okinawa with my unit from Hawaii. Extremely intelligent, he earned his Bachelor's, Master's, and Doctorate degrees in Micro-Biology at Ryukyu University while becoming fluent in reading and writing Japanese.

The following morning I was headed back to the Naha Airport for my return trip home to San Diego. I was unable to catch the military flight to Seattle because there were some mechanical issues with the plane and it was delayed until that Sunday. That would have taken me past my leave days. I washed clothes and packed the night prior so I just had to wait until my daughter was ready. I really enjoyed myself at home on Okinawa again and I realized then that seven days was just not long enough. I was happy because I was able to see everyone I wanted to see while experiencing Japanese culture again. As I walked around the airport prior to my flight, I made a promise to myself that I would return to Okinawa after retirement and do it all again.

My grandson Idris Naim Siddiq was born the day after I left and at the start of the last ten days of Ramadan. During the last ten days of Ramadan, on one of the odd number days, "Lailatul Qadr" or "Night of Power," would occur where if you prayed during this time, that one night would be worth 1000 months of prayer. It was ironic enough that he was born during the month of Ramadan, but during one of the last ten days was a total blessing. On another note, he was born a month early and was only observed in the Neo-Natal Intensive Care Unit (NICU) for one day. Allahu Ahkbar!

Iftar (Breaking of the Fast) at Camp Pendleton Marine Base

Not fully recovered from the jetlag of my trip to Okinawa, I attended a special Iftar at the invitation of the Muslim Chaplain at Camp Pendleton. He invited all the base Chaplains on the installation, which totaled about 50 but only eight attended. He wanted to give the military leadership the opportunity to experience an Iftar. The senior Chaplain on the base attended after just returning to the west coast that morning. Also in attendance were the Chaplain's Commanding Officer and two Imams, plus a few of their congregation from the Escondido and Temecula Masjids, and the Islamic Center of San Diego. As we waited for the guests to arrive the Chaplain showed us a video that a group from Hollywood produced on him representing the faith and the Navy Chaplain Corps. The meal was catered by the Mystic Grill of La Mesa, California. They provided a wonderful Middle Eastern spread of meats, rice, bread, salad and pastries.

For those that attended, it was a learning experience that I really think that they appreciated. We made sure that we sat Muslims at every table so that we could elaborate on the subjects that were not clear while the

Chaplain explained the different aspects of Ramadan, like fasting, Iftars, Tarawee prayers, charity, and a host of other topics. He spoke until we broke the fast at sunset and then prayed the Maghrib prayer. The Imam from the Islamic Center of San Diego called the adhan (call to prayer), and explained the history of the adhan and what the words meant in English. Once the prayer was finished, we ate dinner and entertained questions from our guests, who sat at our tables. I, along with a few others were interviewed by the Base Public Affairs correspondent that was assigned to cover the event. The event went very well and I think that it left a good impression on the hearts and minds of those who witnessed it.

After my return to San Diego, there were only ten days left in the month of Ramadan. The very next weekend I went to San Antonio for Labor Day and that made the month go by just that much faster. I finished the Quran that weekend and seriously thought about how many times I've finished it during Ramadan. To be honest, I've lost count. Muslims worldwide were starting to gear up for the upcoming three day celebration at the end of Ramadan, Eid Ul Fitr (Feast after the Fast). That year the Eid prayer was held downtown at the San Diego Convention Center. It seemed like every year we had to have a larger location for the prayer because there were so many Muslims attending. I looked forward to the prayer and celebration like I did every year. Insha Allah (God willing) our prayers and fasting were accepted by the creator. Ramadan Mubarak!!!

Don't Assume They're Practicing Muslims

Muslim identity has led me to inquire into many of the names that I came across in the course of my duties. My position allowed me to monitor the incoming and outgoing Marines on the Recruit Depot. I also had access to systems that could generate rosters of all of the Depot personnel. While scrolling down a roster of one of the sections, I noticed a name that appeared to be a Muslim name. I must say that I had a pretty good track record of recognizing Muslim names and better than that, on many occasions I had been able to tell what countries the person in question came from. I loved talking to Muslims in the military to see what type of experiences they had been through. The section was located close to my office so I told myself that I would go to the section to meet the young Marine.

When I went to meet him I told him that I saw his name on a roster and I knew it was a Muslim name. He replied that he was Moroccan. I told him that my family visited Morocco back in 2000 and that it was a great experience for us. I then asked what masjid he attended and he replied that he didn't attend any masjid. I realized then that he was not a practicing Muslim. I didn't ask why but I had seen many cases where practicing Muslims immigrate to the United States and for some reason, they left their Islam back in their countries. Most of the cases had to do with the fact that these individuals felt that life was so much easier not being Muslim. The two main reasons why Muslim men backslid, or didn't practice the religion after being exposed to American culture were the promiscuous women and alcohol. The main two reasons for women were the desire not to wear the hijab, or head covering and the notion that in Islam, women were treated as second class citizens. This misconception primarily came from the cultural practices of the country they came from. What I had noticed was that since 9/11, many Muslims felt threatened by exposing the fact that they were Muslims. After the backlash of attacks and discrimination of 9/11 and the masjid issue at Ground Zero, many Muslims chose to give up their Muslim identity out of fear that they would face retribution if identified as being Muslim. There were still many court cases that involved Muslims who had remained dedicated to their faith and had been forced to quit their jobs because of the harassment and discrimination.

I asked the young Marine what his future plans were and he told me that he was getting out of the Corps in a year. It was brought to my attention a month later that he had received disciplinary action and was demoted due to a driving under the influence (DUI) charge and was found not eligible for reenlistment to remain in the Corps.

On another occasion while scrolling down my inbound personnel roster, I noticed another name that could have been Muslim. I utilized my information system to gain access to his Marine Corps information and his religion reflected "Muslim." I then checked to see what day he was due to arrive at the command. About two weeks after his arrival I called his supervisor and asked if she knew that he was a Muslim. We were in the month of Ramadan and I wanted to ensure that his religious accommodations were being met if requested. His supervisor informed me that she would make sure that he was excused from physical fitness training because we thought that he was fasting and couldn't eat nor drink during daylight hours. She was familiar with Ramadan because of previous Muslims she had served with.

A week later I called him to see if he was interested in attending Friday prayers. Again, I assumed that he was a practicing Muslim. He told me that he was not interested in attending. I asked if he was a practicing Muslim and he told me that he used to be but not anymore. I left the situation alone because I didn't want him to feel that I was harassing him. I'm a firm believer that Allah (swt) holds those accountable for their disobedience to his laws. A week later he received disciplinary action for being intoxicated at the rifle range. He too would have been demoted but due to his financial situation, his Commanding Officer was lenient on him.

These were only two cases where I assumed they were practicing Muslims based on their names. Alcohol was forbidden in Islam and they both disregarded the guidance of the Quran which stated that alcohol and gambling were the handiwork of Shaitan, or Satan. They were both punished by the Marine Corps' Uniformed Code of Military Justice and unless they repented, asked for Allah's (swt) forgiveness, and returned to the straight path, a greater punishment awaited them on the Day of Judgment. Allah (swt) knows best.

Ignorance is not an Excuse

With resources like the internet that we have today, information on anything is available at our fingertips. There was no longer the need to go to the library or bookstore for research on certain topics. A recent incident at work reminded me that regardless of the resources via the information highway, some chose to remain ignorant, rather than utilizing the web to research what was true and not true about Islam.

Last week I received a very disturbing email from a close friend of mine at work. She worked at the opposite end of the hallway. She forwarded an email sent to her from a friend of hers who worked at the Depot Human Resources Office, an office whose personnel should be highly trained in cultural diversity and familiar with religious practices. My friend knew that I was Muslim but at that time I don't think that her friend knew. The email contained a video of a woman being kicked and stoned by a circle of angry citizens. It was very graphic as the helpless woman just absorbed stones with her body while trying to avoid an onslaught of whaling kicks from the bystanders. I couldn't determine what country they were from but my intuition was leaning toward either Afghanistan or Iran. They might not have even been Muslims.

Her misled friend stated in her email that the woman was being stoned to death because she refused to marry the man that her parents had arranged for her to marry. That was probably not true because in Islam the woman has the right not to marry the man chosen for her. She also stated some very derogatory comments about Islam and asked her friend, "What type of religion from God would allow this," and "How is Islam a religion of peace?" Contrary to what she might have thought, that stoning was a Christian and Islamic practice in the early days of the prophets but it was a cultural practice depending on the geographical area.

As I had mentioned several times while writing this book, many countries combine cultural practices with the religion, knowing that it was not permissible to do so. Those on the outside would then interpret that type of behavior to be Islamic. I replied back to my friend by saying that I was just as appalled as she was after viewing the video. I also explained to her that her friend should not blame that behavior on Islam. I went to the internet and Googled "stoning in the Bible," and retrieved two verses from the Bible in Psalms relating "to stoning women who are adulterers." I did this just to show her that stoning was done in earlier times for wrongdoers. It took about two minutes to retrieve this information. I sent these verses to my friend and asked her to send it to her friend who sent her the video. I mentioned in the email that unless she researched this information before sending it to all of her email contacts she should have refrained from sending it. Furthermore, on a military installation, we were not permitted to send these types of emails on government computers. This was a very serious offense that could have led to termination or suspension of computer access. I chose not to report her friend. That would've really given her a negative attitude toward Islam.

My friend sensed that I was upset about the email and apologized for sending it to me. I told her that I wasn't mad and that I was glad that she sent it because it gave me the opportunity to explain a little about Islam and I offered to sit down with her and her friend to dialogue about the issue. I also sent her a website about Islam and asked if she would explore it for any questions that she had about the religion. Muslims have learned through experience that talking about these issues with non-Muslims gave them a totally different outlook on the religion of Islam. By opening the doors of masjids around the country to non-Muslims, they got the opportunity to see how we worshiped and they could ask questions right from the source. Needless to say, I didn't receive a reply back from either of the two.

The next day as I walked up to the corridor to enter the building that I work in, I came face to face with the culprit that sent the email. She couldn't look me in the face. As she walked by she stared down at the ground and I sensed the embarrassment in her. I spoke to her and asked how she was doing. She replied that she was doing fine.

Enclosed in one of my emails to my friend, I mentioned that with the internet, there is no excuse for anyone to say that they didn't know about a certain subject. All that it took was the will or desire to know. If she would've researched the information contained in the video, would that have changed her mind about circulating the video? Or, was it just her hatred toward Islam that triggered the reaction? With so much demonization of Islam taking place today due to the masjid project at ground zero, or a series of bombing threats, I can see how the latter choice would be the best course of action for her. Hopefully she used this incident as a learning experience and it had motivated her to learn more about Islam, just in a sense to show her that you can't blame the entire religion for the actions of a small group.

The Afshar Hospital in Kabul, Afghanistan

On October 16, 2010, I attended a presentation at the Islamic Center that really opened my eyes to the poverty, helplessness, and lack of health awareness facing the people of Afghanistan. I had witnessed news reports and specials televised describing the conditions in the region, but to hear it from a doctor who was there two weeks ago, it really hit home. We took for granted here in America something very simple like a hospital existing every five to ten miles, and the quality of care we receive here. Well in Afghanistan, the Afshar Hospital in the capital city of Kabul could be compared to the ninth wonder of the world. Its existence made an indelible impact on Afghan society, where the life expectancy of both males and females was only forty-two years old, as reported by the World Health Organization.

Due to the generosity of a wealthy family from Fresno, California, the Afghan ninth wonder of the world existed. The American Medical Overseas Relief (AMOR) was responsible for its existence. What started as an idea in 2002, had now become a vital instrument that would help to provide some stability in a country that was unstable well before the Afghan war with the Soviets. After three years of construction and a four million dollar price tag, the hospital opened in April of 2009. This was after numerous meetings with the local religious leaders, community leaders, and families. They've asked for corporate help throughout the United States but none of the corporations were willing to risk funds in war-torn Afghanistan.

The hospital was built by Afghans for Afghans and had an all Afghan staff. There were 15 resident doctors and out of those 15, three were women. The resident doctors were chosen from the brightest medical students at Kabul University. In Afghanistan you can become a doctor after four years of college so they were somewhat unqualified per United States standards. AMOR required additional training in order for them to become certified doctors. In their first month of operation, they treated over 3000 patients. The organization had received calls from doctors throughout the Middle East including Iran and Turkey that wanted to become a part of the staff but AMOR only wanted to utilize Afghan doctors to care for their people. The Residency Program along with the Community Outreach and Education Program have made a substantial impact on saving the lives of many Afghan women and children and have served as a lifeline to brighten the future of a country that had experienced darkness under rule of the Taliban. One woman had had eight pregnancies and none of the babies survived. She delivered her ninth baby at the Afshar Hospital with no complications.

The doctor that gave the presentation, also a Fresno native, was asked to become a part of the AMOR organization, a non-profit organization sponsored by the family. The doctor traveled to Kabul seven times and had another trip planned for the following week. As security will always be a threat to Americans in Afghanistan, the doctor was escorted by two armed guards, around the clock, once he touched Afghan soil.

During the presentation, the doctor mentioned that Kabul was becoming pretty modern after the arrival of the coalition forces. He related that poverty was rampant in the capital city that was built in the 1930s for 500,000 people but now was home to over five million. Many of the streets were covered with trash and the sewage system was very inadequate or non-existent. He went on to explain that Afghanistan was a nomadic country and that the sheep and goat herders had the right to lay claim to any part of the city they wanted. He showed a photo of some goat herders and their livestock that had set up their tents in the middle of the city. After a few more slides, he showed a photo of a man spraying sewage off the sidewalk with an AK-47 strapped to his back. These photos illustrated two of the many extremes experienced in Afghanistan.

There were two vital statistics that caught the attention of the Fresno natives. Forty percent of all Afghan children died before the age of five and one out of every four women died due to complications related to pregnancy. These two statistics were the catalysts that touched their hearts to make a change in Afghanistan. Most alarming of the statistics done on infant immortality was that most of them were dying from preventable and treatable illnesses like tuberculosis, diarrhea, and respiratory infections. Women were dying from poor nutrition, no prenatal care, poor hygiene, and complications of pregnancy and delivery.

Two monumental tasks that the hospital staff encountered were producing birth certificates and establishing contact information for their patients. Birth certificates were not issued in Afghanistan prior to the opening of the hospital. When the staff asked their first patients when they were born, the response was, "I was born after the big flood but before the Soviet invasion." The hospital administrative staff now issued a birth certificate for every child born. With Afghanistan being so rural and mountainous, many had no addresses for the staff to contact them for follow-up appointments. The staff now utilized directions and cell phones to maintain contact.

Not only had the hospital improved the mental and physical condition of the people of Afghanistan, it also started to implement some cultural change. When the doctor first walked into the hospital, the women on the staff would jump to one side of the hallway and stare down at the ground, avoiding eye contact with him. He stated that now when he walks in, they yell and wave to him from down the hallway.

The intent of the presentation was to motivate individuals to provide long term support for the hospital. Paying $3 for pre-natal care, 60 cents for a week's worth of a child's antibiotics, or $150 for labor and delivery, were a fraction of what you paid for those services in other countries. Eighty-five percent of all donations went directly to the hospital. Donations of any size meant the difference between life and death in Afghanistan. Although there was an announcement for the presentation the day prior after Friday prayers, only 20 people showed for the presentation and maybe one of them was Afghan. We as a Muslim community must do more to ease the suffering of those who are less fortunate than we are.

Their Spiritual Journey to Mecca

It had been the subject of many conversations that we have had since meeting in Okinawa, Japan in 2005. As I told them about my experience at Hajj, their faces always lit up and I could always hear the excitement in their voices and feel the envy of one day being able to experience the fifth pillar of Islam themselves. The former Navy couple both separated from the Navy because military life was not conducive to a rewarding Islamic lifestyle. There were so many negative distractions that they encountered while serving, that it convinced them to choose other careers. This was in addition to the fact that they wanted to start a family and have the wife stay home to look after their children. He, of Filipino descent and she of Mexican descent, were two of the most God-fearing, un-materialistic, and humble Muslims that I have ever met. From the southern Philippines, he often told me stories about how it was growing up there. His wife came from a strict Catholic family that held steady to the Catholic traditions. I did not know of a more deserving family to make the Pilgrimage. The Pilgrimage to Mecca was a spiritual transformation for Muslims. I myself am a witness to how it has changed the lives of many Muslims.

Working two jobs and sometimes three, he was able to pay off all of his debts and save enough money to defray the cost of the Hajj for four people. The Hajj program this year sponsored by an organization from Orange County, California, ran roughly about $6,000.00 a person. The task came at a price because working three jobs deprived him of the time he could've spent with his family and left his wife fending for the kids about twenty-one of twenty-four hours a day. In addition to the hours, switching from night shift to day shift on a weekly basis grossly affected his sleep pattern that he hadn't been able to regulate in over two years.

Although they had watched videos and television shows that featured the Pilgrimage to Mecca, the shows left out many details relating to the experience. For that reason, they both took advantage of every opportunity to hear about the journey first hand. This gave them a good idea of how to negotiate the physical and spiritual trek across the sands of Saudi Arabia. A major concern of theirs was the fact that they were taking their two children who were two and a half years and eleven months old. As I had explained to them, Hajj was a grueling experience for adults so the children would make it that much more difficult. In order to alleviate some of the difficulty, they were accompanied by his mother to help with the children. She had traveled from the east coast to meet them for the trip. This way, she too would be able to fulfill her obligation of being one of the guests of Allah (swt) at Hajj.

I met with them a week prior to their journey at the Muslim restaurant Casa Medina, where they both collected prayers from the local community to say when they reached Mount Arafat. Any prayer that was said on Arafat would be answered by Allah (swt). I also had lunch with them the day prior to their departure and they were overwhelmed with excitement about going. I looked forward to hearing about their experience in about 21 days when they returned.

I received a call from the brother two days after they returned to San Diego. The trip went well other than the fact that they were all sick, including his mother. We planned to meet a week later to sit down and discuss the details. The next Friday I ran into him at the masjid during Friday prayers and we agreed to meet that Sunday at their place.

The visit started with viewing videos that he took with his phone. Cameras were not allowed at the Prophet Muhammad's (Pbuh) Masjid in Madinah or Masjid Al-Haram in Mecca. If caught taking photos, the Saudi guards would either confiscate your film or they would not let you enter. This was done to deter pilgrims from taking photos at the holy sites and selling them for profit. Most of them were one to two minute videos that captured key moments during their Hajj experience.

As they started from the time they arrived in Jeddah, I could recall and relate to a great deal of what they talked about. The registration lines were long, and the pilgrims processing had little or no patience. That was probably because everyone was anxious to get to Mecca. Unlike my experience in 1999, they went straight from Jeddah to Mecca by bus and then flew into Madinah. We were bused to Madinah and subsequently bused to Mecca. Most of those making Hajj go to Madinah first to conduct forty prayers in the Prophet Muhammad's (Pbuh) Masjid and then on to Mecca for the Hajj. This leg of the trip was not a part of the Hajj.

As we talked, my sister poured me some Zam Zam water that they brought back and served some of the specific dates that the Prophet Muhammad (Pbuh) used to eat. Zam Zam water came from the original well that Hagar and her son Ishmael drank from after being sent into the desert by Abraham. During my Hajj experience, the water was piped underground from Masjid Al-Haram, the place where the actual spring came up in the desert.

Once they reached the city of Mecca they glanced over and through buildings for the opportunity to see the masjid. From that point, they remained full of anticipation about the chance to finally see Masjid Al-Haram, and actually pray in it. Once the masjid appeared in the open, they were overwhelmed with emotions, just as I was when I got my first view of it. The masjid was a focal point that over 1.2 billion Muslims prayed toward, five times a day, every day. The structure of the masjid housed the first Islamic House of God (Ka'bah), built by Prophets Abraham and his son Ishmael.

While in Mecca, awaiting transportation to Madinah, they stayed in the Hilton Hotel across the street from Masjid Al-Haram. That made it easy for them to access at any time of the morning or night. During the Hajj it is highly unlikely to not find the masjid crowded. With the usual two million plus pilgrims, and the Ka'bah as the center of attraction, the masjid was even full at two and three o'clock in the morning. This year there were an estimated 2.4 million registered pilgrims, and another two million unregistered. Traveling anywhere in Mecca was time consuming.

After their group sponsor coordinated their transportation to Madinah, they had to wait twelve hours before they could actually load the plane and depart. The wait was indicative to what they had been told about the Pilgrimage.

While they were in Madinah, they stayed at a hotel in the vicinity of the Prophet Muhammad's (Pbuh) Masjid. The hotel was arranged by the company that sponsored the trip. This made it convenient for them to visit the masjid at any time. They were also able to visit some of the famous sites in Medina such as the mountain where the Battle of Uhud took place and the grave site of the Prophet's (Pbuh) Uncle Hamza.

Everywhere they went the people were marveled at the fact that they brought their two children to Hajj. A few that inquired about the couple were amazed that they were once in the Navy. The Hajj rituals were tough enough for the two of them, let alone the two babies. Everyone jumped at the opportunity to play with them, especially the workers who were in Saudi just for employment and left their families in their respective countries.

They both were fascinated about the size of the Prophet Muhammad's (Pbuh) Masjid. The masjid is about six blocks long and entertains a constant flow of worshippers, regardless of what time it was. Some just lived in the masjid for eight days while they conducted the daily five prayers. These were the worshippers that were fortunate to pray in the first row behind the Imam. The closer you were to the front of the masjid for prayer, the more blessings you received. Also, the early arrivers had a better chance of walking by the Prophet Muhammad's (Pbuh) tomb. After one of the prayers, my brother was able to come within ten feet of it. The entire masjid was carpeted including the roof. I found it a lot healthier to pray on the roof because the open air made you less vulnerable to the germs of the sick worshippers. The majority of the masjid is closed in and once you enter, you can hear the coughing and sneezing throughout the structure.

Once their duties were fulfilled in Madinah, they departed to Mecca for the Hajj. It was arranged for them to stay in a small apartment close to Jabal Al-Nur (Mountain of Light). Their bus stopped along the way at a station where they obtained the state of ihram, which was to put on the two pieces of white cloth that they would wear throughout the Hajj.

Traveling the different stages of the Hajj for them was grueling. The heat, sleep deprivation, hunger, and waiting in bus lines was enough to cause anyone to loose their sanity. Mentally, they were well prepared for the trip. They knew what to expect and they took every challenge in stride. Patience was one of the key virtues of Hajj and it was definitely tested during the journey.

What they didn't anticipate, was the help they received from a Muslim Vietnamese couple and an Indonesian brother married to a Vietnamese sister that came to their aid while they struggled with their children, their stroller, and communicating with the locals. The Vietnamese couple, who spoke Arabic, were studying at the University of Mecca, and the other couple had traveled from Fresno, California to make the Hajj. My brother alluded that it was a blessing to have the four of them there, and they considered them as angels that appeared out of nowhere.

As they traveled through the cities of Mina, Arafat, and Muzdalifah, things didn't get any easier. By that time, all five of them had gotten sick and one of the babies had to go to the emergency room. My brother was escorted to a clinic where he and his daughter were immediately seen. It took all of ten minutes to diagnose both of them. It was no cost to him because all medical services were free in Saudi Arabia. They pressed on through the Hajj rituals realizing that this could be a once in a lifetime journey. They still kept everything in perspective, while reflecting back on why they were there in the first place, to complete the Hajj and have it accepted by Allah (swt). For a family that sacrificed so much to get there, the conditions couldn't get bad enough for them to get discouraged. They were focused on whatever it took to complete the Hajj.

Once the Hajj was completed and they processed out of Jeddah, they had to endure the long three-stop trip back through Germany, North Carolina, and then San Diego. Physically and mentally exhausted, they both tried to sleep whenever the babies would let them. It was a good feeling to relax for a while without the hustle and bustle, and worrying about where they had to be next.

He told me about their mixed feelings of leaving Mecca. It was a spiritual blessing to be in the land where Islam originated and to walk in perhaps some of the same pathways of the Prophet Muhammad (Pbuh), but with all that they encountered during the Pilgrimage, they were ready to depart for home.

They were so thankful for the opportunity to make Hajj. Prayerfully they fulfilled all of the obligations of the Hajj and that their Hajj would be accepted. Now they had completed the five pillars of Islam. What awaited them would be a decision made on Judgment Day for them to enter Jannah (Paradise).

Passing on the Torch

While I looked forward to retirement, I knew that I left the Corps in the hands of those well prepared for the challenges ahead. As evident by the Corps' recruiting statistics, high quality men and women were stepping up to the challenge of becoming U. S. Marines, and they were entering our ranks stronger, smarter, and motivated.

From the day I stepped onto those yellow footprints at Parris Island, until the time when I've watched my last Recruit Graduation Ceremony here in San Diego, I find it rewarding and ironic to have had touched the soil on both Depots. One was at the beginning of my career and the other at the end. Although there were still debates about which Depot was the best, they both continued to carry out the mission by recruiting and making Marines.

My thirty years on active duty has been a great experience that has allowed me to come into contact with both, dedicated military members from all branches, and pious Muslims from all over the world. In one aspect, my service was about defending the freedom that we as Americans deserved, and the other was a cultural and spiritual enlightenment. Both the Corps and the Islamic community had introduced me to influential leaders that inspired me to perpetuate my allegiance to the world's finest fighting force and to God, the Creator of all things.

The Corps' leadership maintains that the Corps will continue to focus on four key issues; (1) America needs an expeditionary force in readiness, (2) the Corps needs better trained and educated Marines, (3) the Corps remains committed to taking care of Sailors, Marines and their families, and (4) the Corps will send our best trained and equipped Sailors and Marines to fight the war in Afghanistan. These issues along with the Corps' focus on honor, courage, and commitment have been echoed at every level whenever Marines and Sailors were gathered in numbers. There was no doubt in my mind that the Navy and Marine Corps team would continue to carry on the legacy of our Corps.

Although I'll no longer deploy, stand the watch, participate in a Post and Relief ceremony, or witness another of my troops being promoted, I verbally solidify my lifelong commitment and allegiance to the Corps, and I share that same allegiance to the Creator of the Heavens, the Earth, and all that is in between.

Semper Fidelis
And
Peace be unto You

EPILOGUE

As I hang up the uniform, I reflect back on the progress that the Marine Corps has made in providing an environment that is void of harassment, discrimination, and prejudice. This accomplishment would lead one to believe that Muslims in the military stood a good chance of not being subjected to either. Yet, we're still experiencing problems with our low ranking Muslim Sailors, Airmen, Soldiers, and Marines at some of the lower echelon units that could have been avoided.

With the ongoing war with Afghanistan, the Israeli/Palestinian conflict, the increasing numbers of Muslim immigrants migrating to the United States, and an occasional arrest of so-called Muslims facing apprehension by law enforcement officials for trying to detonate a bomb somewhere to kill innocent people, the backlash against Muslims, whether innocent or not, will continue. What makes one accept fanaticism and become filled with hatred and violence? I can only speculate, because I have never met any Muslims with those views. I have been fortunate enough to have met Muslims from many corners of the earth and not once has that mentality been displayed toward me or my fellow Americans.

Overall I feel that most of the American people realize that Muslims in the military maintain our allegiance to America and we also support and defend the constitution of the United States of America. Sadly said, the ignorance and hatred of the religion of Islam will probably always exist in America.

Lastly, our world has been experiencing floods, earthquakes, abnormal temperatures, pestilence, and other natural disasters, along with famine, genocide, human uprisings, and economic instability. These are not occurring by coincidence. God is not pleased with the conditions of his people and these are only signs of his displeasure. Like he has demonstrated in the days of the prophets, he has wiped out entire societies and replaced them with a new people to do his will. Out of his mercy and beneficence, he has spared us thus far but only he knows when enough is enough. At this point in time it's not too late to change our hearts and minds and focus on those things that are pleasing to him. Let us worship God and worship him alone without partners. Let's take care of the homeless, the orphans, our parents, and those less fortunate than we are. Let's love our neighbors and treat people the way that we want to be treated. Let's not spend excessively, overeat, or spend out of our means. Finally, let us have the desire to learn about the heritage, languages, and cultures of the different people we have on this planet called earth. It can only make it a better world to live in, Ameen.

Peace be unto you

ABOUT THE AUTHOR

Hafiz Naim Ali Camp was born on 7 December 1957 as Michel Andre' Camp into a military family in Verdun, France. He changed his name after becoming Muslim. Growing up in France, Germany, and different bases throughout the United States, made him accustomed to a lifestyle that many never get the opportunity to experience. The author attended public schools in Newport News, Virginia and started his college education at Virginia State College, now Virginia State University in Petersburg, Virginia. In 1981, after the second semester, he enlisted in the Marine Corps.

He worked his way through the ranks and in July 2005 he obtained the highest enlisted rank obtainable in his career path: Master Gunnery Sergeant. During his career he served with six major commands, two of those commands being infantry units and one artillery unit. He spent over eleven years in Okinawa, Japan.

Through the different relationships he experienced in his career, he developed a passion for different cultures and a strong sense of cultural diversity. He completed his BS in Sociology at the University of Maryland.

For a period of 30 years, he took advantage of the opportunity to serve with countless dedicated Sailors, Airmen, Soldiers, Coast Guardsmen, and some of the world's finest Marines.

He and his wife have four children and two grandchildren. They now reside in San Antonio, Texas.

Semper Fidelis

REFERENCE

American Bible Society, The Bible, Revised Standard Version (New York 1971), 1067, iv Preface

Collections of hadith by Sahih Al-Bukhari, Sahih Muslim, Imam Al-Nasai and Imam Ahmad

GLOSSARY

Term	Definition
Adhan	Call to prayer
Al Aqabah	Largest of the stone pillars or Jamarats
Al Fatihah	The opening prayer in the Quran
Al Jazeerah	Middle Eastern News Station
Allahu Ahkbar	God is Great
Al Safa & Al Marwa	Two small mountains located in Masjid Al Haram
Ameen	Amen
Arafat	A place next to Mecca visited by Pilgrims during Hajj
Asr	Late afternoon prayer
Bid'ah	Innovation
Burka	All-enveloping cloak worn by some Muslim women
Cobra Gold	Military exercise in Thailand
Deen	The practice of Islam
Dhuhr	Early afternoon prayer
Dirhams	Moroccan currency
DMZ	Demilitarized Zone, buffer zone between North and South Korea

Eid Ul Adha	Feast after Hajj
Eid Ul Fitr	Feast after the Fast
Fajr	Morning prayer
Hadith	Things Prophet Muhammad (Pbuh) said and actions he did
Hafith	One who memorized the Quran
Halal	Islamically slaughtered meat
Hajj	Pilgrimage to Mecca
Head	Marine bathroom
Hijab	Women's head covering
Iftar	Meal for breaking the fast
Ihram	Two pieces of white cloth worn during Hajj
Isha	Evening prayer
Jabal Al Nur	Mountain of Light
Jallaba	Long Moroccan robe with a hood
Jamarats	Pillars stoned during the Hajj
Jannah	Paradise
Jedda	City in Saudi Arabia
Ka'bah	Structure in the center of Masjid Al Haram
Khateeb	Person who gives the khutbah or sermon
Khutbah	Friday sermon
Kufee	Head covering for men
Lailatul Qadr	Night of power
Madrassa	Islamic School
Maghrib	Early evening prayer
Mimbar	Pulpit in the masjid where the Imam gives the khutbah
Nikab	Conservative head covering to a woman's face
Portholes	Marine and Navy term for windows
Quarterdeck	A section in the squadbay

Qiblah	Direction that Muslims pray
Rakah	Unit of prayer
Ramadan	Ninth month of Islamic calendar
Roppongi	Section of Tokyo
Riyals	Saudi Arabian currency
Sadaqah	Charity
Sahabah	Companions of Prophet Muhammad (Pbuh)
Salat	Prayer
Semper Fidelis	Always faithful
Shahadah	Declaration of faith
Shaitan	Satan
Shalwar Khamees	Pakistani outfit
Shi'ites	Sect of Islam
Singapore Sling	Famous alcoholic drink of Singapore
Smokey	Drill Instructor's hat
Squadbay	House for Marine Recruits
Sunnah	Way
Swanxman	Official pledge of Groove phi Groove SFI
(Swt)	Subhanah wa' TaAla, Glory be to God
Tabliqh Jammat	Group traveling to lecture about Islam
Taraweeh	Special prayers during Ramadan
Tawaf	Circling the Ka'bah
Thikr	Remembrance
Ummah	Community
Witr	Extra
Zakat	Formal charity during Ramadan
Zam Zam	Water from the well of Masjid Al Haram

www.ingramcontent.com/pod-product-compliance
Ingram Content Group UK Ltd.
Pitfield, Milton Keynes, MK11 3LW, UK
UKHW041946190726
13854UKWH00004B/1828

9 781426 958229